the mba jungle

B–SCHOOL
SURVIVAL
GUIDE

the mba jungle

B-SCHOOL
SURVIVAL
GUIDE

Jon Housman

. . . .

and the *MBA Jungle* Editors

jungle
interactive media inc.

PERSEUS PUBLISHING

Cambridge, Massachusetts

-01

Copyright © 2001 by Jon Housman and MBA Jungle

Cataloging-in-Publication Data is available from the Library of Congress
ISBN 0–7382-0511-7

Perseus Publishing is a member of the Perseus Books Group.
Find us on the World Wide Web at http://www.perseuspublishing.com
Perseus Publishing books are available at special discounts for bulk purchases in the U.S. by corporations, institutions, and other organizations. For more information, please contact the Special Markets Department at the Perseus Books Group, 11 Cambridge Center, Cambridge, MA 02142, or call (617)252-5298.

Text design by Jeffrey P. Williams
Set in 11-point Janson Text by Perseus Publishing Services

First printing, September 2001

1 2 3 4 5 6 7 8 9 10—03 02 01

contents

mba jungle
contributors

The portions of this book that have appeared previously either in *MBA Jungle* or on mbajungle.com have been modified or updated since their original publication. A special thanks to these and other contributors.

"What's the Payoff?" by Corey Hajim
"Seven Tips to Make Part-Time Work for You,"
    by Sheila Resari
"The Dual Degree: Two for One Special,"
    by Mark Murray
"Women on the Verge," by Farah Miller
"Getting into the School You Want," by Robyn Gearey
"Understanding the GMAT," by Alicia Abell
"The Man Behind the GMAT," by S. Kirk Walsh
"What to Bring to the Party," by Deirdre O'Scannlain
"Six Things You Can Leave at Home,"
    by Justin Heimberg
"My Grades Depend on Them!" by Jeff Ousborne
"When Teammates Attack," by Sasha Shapiro
"Ten Ways to Annoy Your Teammates,"
    by Justin Heimberg

"It's Not What You Said," by David Blend

"Six Things Not to Do in an Interview,"
   by Justin Heimberg

"Hot for Teacher," by Jeff Ousborne

"Why Your Resumé Got Tossed," by Sara Goldsmith

"The Ultimate Recruiting Playbook," by David Blend

"Disaster Relief: Survival Strategies for
   Recruiting Calamities," by Russell Wild

"Interviews Gone Bad," by David Blend and
   Alexis Offen

"Jobhunters from Hell," by David Blend and
   Alexis Offen

"Leaving the Perfect Voicemail Message,"
   by Paul Scott

"Dining for Dollars," by Paul Scott

"The Take-Away: Lessons from B-School's Best Minds,"
   by Russell Wild

"Nine Things That Are Not as Important to Remember," by Justin Heimberg

"Stepping Up," by David Blend, Anne Dunham,
   Jacob Kalish, Maria Spinella, and Dirk Standen

the mba jungle

B-SCHOOL
SURVIVAL
GUIDE

1

The Art of Success

···

IT'S HAPPENED. BUSINESS CULTURE AND POPULAR CULTURE ARE IN-
SEPARABLE THESE DAYS. CEOS ARE COUNTED AMONG TODAY'S
CELEBRITIES, AND THE AVERAGE PERSON IS EQUALLY FAMILIAR WITH
Alan Greenspan and Al Green, as familiar with the Dow
Jones as with Catherine Zeta-Jones. When General Elec-
tric's CEO Jack Welch decided to write his memoirs, he was
promptly advanced more money for his book contract than
Ronald Reagan, Britney Spears, Colin Powell, and the pope
were for theirs.

Business is everywhere. No one's surprised anymore when
the guy at the deli counter offers stock tips, or when the
teenagers making your Frappuccino are arguing about the
Microsoft antitrust case. CNBC is in with the hip crowds, and
Grandma checks in with the market as often as she does the
weather. Business has become the fastest growing major in
undergraduate institutions, and campuses buzz with glorious
stories of students who didn't even stick around to graduate
before making their fortune. Indeed, business achievement is
the new yardstick of success in today's society.

In many ways, business school is at the center of this cultural phenomenon. For some, B-school is the passport to the
boardroom, the ticket to the top of the corporate ladder. Just
as the Federal Reserve Bank churns out newly minted $100
bills, B-schools pump out the new generation of business
leaders by the hundreds of thousands. They are the pipeline

of raw material with which the nation's—and the world's—leading businesses build the future. And MBAs are not limited to the traditional corporate world: From Wall Street to Madison Avenue, from Sand Hill Road to 1600 Pennsylvania Avenue, today's MBAs lead organizations large and small, in every conceivable industry. They are the executives and entrepreneurs who power the economy.

So it's hardly surprising that business school applications have been on a huge upswing for the past twenty years, to the point where some elite schools receive about ten applications for every available spot in the class. This is also why salaries of B-school grads have risen spectacularly: According to *Business Week*, compensation for students graduating from the top thirty B-schools averages $127,000. That figure represents over three times what the average American *family* makes in a year. It is also an 82-percent increase over what the same students made before starting B-school, and it puts them solidly in the top 1 percent of earners in the world. Oh, did we mention that this salary is just for the first year after graduation?

What does this kind of earning power mean? Simply put, the finest of everything. Trips to exotic destinations, sleek cars, vacation homes, gorgeous jewelry, clothes, electronics, and on and on. But, of course, that's just the materialistic side of the equation. The real payoff is being able to navigate the obstacles and surmount the challenges you face. That could mean starting a company and taking it public, turning around a failing division, or leading a nonprofit and increasing the number of people it serves. It's about being smart, efficient, and creative. It's about the art of success.

The decision to go to business school requires an investment. A big investment. The best schools, as you probably already know, are not inexpensive. And the investment of your time is just as important—maybe more important—as the money required for tuition. But there are no better investments than the ones you make in yourself. And so the question is this: How do you get the greatest return on your investment? That is where the *MBA Jungle B-School Survival Guide* comes in. The book you hold in your hands will help you get the most out of your MBA. From choosing the right school to selecting the right classes, from working well with your classmates to building relationships with your professors, from Day One to the day you get a job offer, the *Survival Guide* will help you get ahead in the business world . . . and have fun along the way.

To B-School or Not to B-School? (A Diagnostic Quiz)

....

MAYBE YOU ALWAYS KNEW YOU WERE GOING TO GO AFTER YOUR MBA. ON THE OTHER HAND, MAYBE THE THOUGHT OCCURRED TO YOU ONLY AFTER YOU WERE PASSED OVER FOR A PROMOTION. OR DID YOU BEGIN your career in PR or nonprofit work but later become interested in banking or marketing? It's also possible that you were always interested in these fields but didn't know how to break into them. Perhaps you've read about the enormous salaries MBAs command. Or maybe you wanted to lead the meetings instead of just sit in them.

To be sure, the upside is extremely attractive. Still, it makes a good deal of sense to ask yourself why you want to go to business school and whether now is the right time. With that in mind, break out your No. 2 pencil and take this little should-I-go-to-B-school quiz, which we have cleverly titled:

TO B OR NOT TO B?

1. Do you envision B-school as a break from your sixty-hour workweek?
2. How do you handle competition?
3. Have you calculated the opportunity costs of not working for the better part of two years?
4. Are you planning on switching careers?

5. Do you want to improve your quantitative business skills?
6. Do you want to diversify your skill set?
7. Do you like taking quizzes that ask you if you like taking quizzes?
8. Do you want to be an entrepreneur?
9. How do you handle working in teams?
10. Are you happy in your job? Are you learning the skills you need to get ahead? Do you have some great opportunities right in front of you?
11. How often do you steal a glance at the corner office?

Okay, put your pencil down. Anywhere is fine. Let's look at these questions a little more closely, because the way you answered them can tell you a lot about whether B-school is for you and whether now is the right time.

1. Do you envision B-school as a break from your sixty-hour workweek?

The working world can be rough, but B-school can be brutal. The programs are rigorous and highly competitive, and they demand your full attention for nearly two years. It's true, your schedule will have huge gaps of "free" time in the middle of the day, but chances are you'll be eyeballing some formula, practicing your interview skills, or reading about why Company X merged with Company Y—and why neither of these companies could come up with more creative names.

In short, this is not college.

2. How do you handle competition?

Business school can be quite competitive. You compete for grades, of course, but also for airtime in class, and for jobs during recruiting season. And not just with your classmates, but with the best and brightest from around the country. If you like competition, well, you'll do fine. But if it makes your skin crawl, you may want to rethink your decision or at least talk to B-school graduates and get a better sense of how you'd fit in.

3. Have you calculated the opportunity costs of not working for the better part of two years?

A lot of people look at the tuition numbers, estimate the cost of renting an apartment, calculate the cost of groceries, books, some new clothes, a bit of entertainment here and there, and think that's the bottom line. It isn't. You also have to calculate what is called the opportunity costs. We're talking about the opportunity costs of leaving the workforce for the better part of two years. In that time, how much salary are you *not* bringing in? How much are you *not* adding to your 401(k)? What will health insurance cost when your company is no longer paying for it? And where would you be in two years if you stayed with your current company? If the answer is the corner office—or damn close to it—well, that's something to weigh.

While stopping the paychecks and commencing the tuition bills is painful, you need to balance it against the quality of the investment and the payback. How much payback? *Business Week* estimated that graduates of the 2000 class would be getting a whopping 82-percent average increase in their salary—and that's just for the first year out! *Forbes* calculated that you can expect at least $100,000 in incremental salary over five years. (*Martha Stewart Living* didn't comment one way or the other.) And don't forget, there are ways to mitigate the near-term financial pain. You can count on making good money during your summer off—about $30,000 over the course of three months. Also, many firms offer tuition reimbursement and generous signing bonuses, and they pay at the time you sign, which is generally during the second year of school.

4. Are you planning to switch careers?

If the answer is yes, B-school is usually a good idea. If the answer is yes, and the career you want involves banking, consulting, marketing, or venture capital, then pass Go and collect $200. All in all, switching careers is probably the number one reason people go to business school—and it is a great reason. Getting your MBA will not only provide you with an entry into to these coveted jobs, but you will also meet dozens of peers who have actually worked in these very industries—and they'll be happy to give you the who, what, when, where, and how. Additionally, if you're planning on going to school full-time, then you have the summer in between the first and second year to do an "internship" in your industry of choice. (Note: Internship is in quotations only because the traditional idea of what an internship consists of should be thrown out the window. You will be paid, and paid well. And you won't likely be going on coffee runs. More on this later.)

5. Do you want to improve your quantitative business skills?

B-schoolers have a name for people who come with little or no analytic skills. That name is "poet." A history major who worked in marketing. An English major who went to a PR firm. Basically, if you can spell "abacus" but can't use one, you're a poet. You get the idea. First of all, if you are a poet, don't worry about it. The "soft" skills you do have (e.g., strong communication, good management) are at least as important as being able to process derivatives. Also, B-schools look to poets to bring diversity to the group—so to some extent, you are in demand. However, it is true that at many jobs, having some quant skills will balance your other talents and take you to the next level. Business school will provide you with this quantitative skill set.

6. Do you want to diversify your skill set?

You may know with certainty that bond trading is all you ever want to do in your career. But if you aren't so sure, B-school is a good opportunity to learn about other pastures. Not just learn, but be qualified to graze there should you choose, or should the economy sour on your current industry . . . or should we run out of cow metaphors.

7. Do you like taking quizzes that ask you if you like taking quizzes?

Let's move on, shall we?

8. Do you want to be an entrepreneur?

Many entrepreneurs or would-be entrepreneurs think twice about getting an MBA because they are under the impression the degree prepares you for corporate life rather than entrepreneurial life. Not true. There are many skills you need as an entrepreneur that you can develop in B-school.

> *Leadership.* Business school is a leadership laboratory, and a great way for you to develop and hone your skills as well as shake hands with big-league CEOs.
>
> *Focus.* Being an entrepreneur means constantly having to cut through the clutter and focus on the important must-do stuff. Ditto for succeeding at B-school.
>
> *Problem-solving skills and grace under pressure.* Again, B-school is a great training ground. And those quantitative skills will come in handy.
>
> *Teamwork.* That's right, cowboy. Even as an entrepreneur you are *always* working with a group. You may be the leader of the group, but knowing how to communicate goals and spark effective teamwork may be the single most important factor in your business's success. Any successful entrepreneur will tell you this.

Of course, there are exceptions. You may feel like you are already good enough in all of these things, or you may have an idea that's too hot to wait on. But as a rule, you will do better as an entrepreneur if you have invested in the MBA.

Yet another reason for this is that in addition to the above skills, B-school gives you lots of other things. Most important among these is networking opportunities. A few years from now, as you consider your start-up, you will know people. Lots of people. People who can invest money in your company, or introduce you to those who can. People who will come work for you. People who know you and may be in a position to become your clients. The network is crucial. Also, having the degree on your resumé is reassuring to would-be investors and employees.

Having said all this, not all MBA programs are created equal—some are much more advanced in their thinking on entrepreneurial matters than others. If you know you want to strike out on your own, you should target a B-school known for its entrepreneur-specific programs, such as those at Wharton, Stanford, Anderson, Stern, and Sloan.

9. How do you handle working in teams?

Cooperative learning is the hallmark of business school. From Day One you will find yourself working as part of a team on all kinds of projects. And yes, your grade depends on the combined work of your team. Obviously, this is great training for the business world, where no one person can succeed on his or her own. But for those who aren't inclined to share and share alike, it can also be a moderately hair-raising experience.

10. Are you happy in your job? Are you learning the skills you need to get ahead? Do you have some great opportunities right in front of you?

If you answered *yes* to these questions, now may not be the right time for you to get your MBA. Nobody is arguing against knowledge for knowledge's sake, but if you don't think you'll be using the kind of skills that B-school teaches, the relative value of spending two years away from your career is exceedingly low. And although post-business-school salaries start in the six figures and go up at a healthy clip, there are folks who are making that and much more *without* a business degree. And yet, and yet . . . a strong case can always be made for gaining skills and meeting people who will help you take the success you have already achieved on your own to an even higher level.

11. How often do you steal a glance at the corner office?

Look to the future. Do you see yourself as a CEO? Managing director? As a leader of a group or division? If the answer is *yes*, this too is a reason to consider an MBA. Of course, B-school most directly trains you and sets you up for your next job. But most MBA programs also train you for your *last* job. Not the job you had previously, but the CEO job you know you want down the road.

In B-school, you will interact with leaders, read about them, debate their tactics and strategies, and, most important, sharpen your own leadership skills in dozens of ways. Not to mention meeting the people who can help you propel your career forward.

A Few Final Thoughts As You Tally Your Score

In the end, business school offers a rare opportunity to take a break from the everyday business world and to focus on the bigger picture and your place in it. To take two years where you are learning new things every day (and most nights). To challenge your accepted notions about business problems and working with people. This part of the experience can be uniquely energizing and is no doubt part of the reason you'll feel like you're ready to conquer the world when you graduate.

A FEW WORDS ABOUT LIFE AFTER B-SCHOOL

Let's gaze into the crystal ball for a moment. Focus on two or three years from now, after you've applied to school, been accepted, worked your butt off, and earned your degree. What comes next? What are your options after you get your MBA? What, in short, is the payoff for your two years of hard work?

Obviously, behind every product and service available in the world there is a business. Which means there's an opportunity for an MBA. Quite literally, the opportunities are limited only by your imagination. From frozen food to luxury cars, from winter coats to wireless technology, from roller skates to fifty-story buildings, from nonprofit organizations to—you get the point. That said, most new B-school grads gravitate to one of the Big Three industries: investment banking, consulting, and marketing.

Investment Banking

Perhaps the most obvious post-MBA choice for diehard number crunchers is investment banking. This can mean a job in corporate finance, sales & trading, equity research, or one of the other positions within an investment bank. All the positions pay extremely well—at top companies, around $150,000 plus a hefty bonus right from the start. At second-tier banks in cities like New York and San Francisco, you're looking at upward of $125,000 plus bonus; in smaller cities, a good starting salary is generally between $100,000 and $125,000.

Here are a few specifics:

As a **corporate finance** associate, you analyze, make projections, and create deal structures. At first, associates gener-

THE PAYOFF

Don't Rush It:
Why Sooner Isn't Always Better

When it comes to entering B-school, timing is everything. A lot of people assume that the more knowledge they get at an early age, the better their chances for success. Who cares if I've only been in the working world for two years? the thinking goes. Why should I wait until I'm twenty-eight, or even twenty-six?

Here's why: Because what you get out of B-school depends on what you *bring* to it. It's not simply about how much work you put in while you are at school. The education you'll receive is not meant to be a lesson in academia. In fact, it's just the opposite—it's a lesson in practicality. The whole point is for you to be able to apply what you learn in your real business life. The transfer of knowledge to some degree depends on your ability to internalize the lessons. When you sit in class, you won't just be taking notes—you'll be thinking to yourself about the time something like that happened to you. You'll experience one of those "Aha!" moments, and with it, a whole new way of approaching similar situations. And the next time something like that does happen you'll recognize it. The truth is, you won't benefit from it nearly as much if you don't bring some of that experience with you into the classroom.

Even if you can live with getting less out of the experience, you should know up front that schools and job recruiters will be skeptical, and you may well face an uphill battle to get into the top schools and to land the coveted jobs.

Of course, there are exceptions to all of this—wunderkind leaders are not completely unheard of—and if you consider yourself one of them, don't let anyone rain on your parade. After all, a guy named Bill Gates didn't even stick around to get his *undergrad* degree.

by Corey Hajim

ally interact with lawyers, create Excel spreadsheets, and . . . little else. Plug and chug becomes a way of life. However, the experience can be intense and instructive, and when you do well, you move up the ladder to higher-level deal structuring and client interactions. After about a year or eighteen months, you gradually get more responsibilities; over the next two years, you do less and less grunt work. Needless to say, this gig is quite lucrative—if the bank has a good year, this is probably the highest-paying job out of B-school.

I-bank option two is **sales & trading**. Traders buy and sell securities and commodities. They arrive well before the market floodgates open (usually between 6:30 and 7:30 A.M.) and collapse around 4:30 P.M. If you enjoy the thrill of high-stakes poker, not to mention managing client relationships, this could be your calling. It's hands-down the best pay-to-working-hour ratio in the business, and lavish client entertainment is typically a must. This is a great option for closers who are early risers and socially inclined. For recent grads, compensation runs about $75,000 to $85,000 a year plus year-end and signing bonuses that can basically double the salary.

The field of **equity research** is considered more cerebral than sales & trading. Here, the goal is to become the expert on an industry or industry subsector—cars, retail, pharmaceuticals, telecom, health care, Latvian knockwurst, whatever. You start as an associate, and twelve-hour days are par for the course. After a few years, you can become a lead analyst in a particular industry, where you get direct exposure to some of the best minds in business: CFOs and other top corporate officers. The pay shoots up as well.

Money management also has its perks: Whether in private client services or portfolio management for a big mutual fund company, you research companies and make investments on behalf of your firm or clients. You might specialize in a niche (e.g., South American large-cap value) or explore whatever strikes your fancy. The work is hard and the competition tough, but strong performers get large amounts of responsibility fast, either at the firm or on their own. This is definitely a field where you can take your track record and go into business for yourself. As for pay, many B-school grads start at about $80,000 plus bonus and move up from there. Fund managers pull in seven figures and get a piece of the action. It's nice to be a fund manager.

Private equity and its subset, **venture capital**, are hot right now. Chances are you'll have to pay your dues in traditional I-banking first, but if you can land a job at a venture capital firm, you can play God with your classmates' business plans. Lots of travel, but the reason is more to meet company management and attend board meetings—unlike a consultant, who may be stuck somewhere for six weeks. In the VC/ private-equity world, your compensation is broken up into salary, bonus, and "carried interest." Salaries generally range from $100,000 to $200,000, and bonuses in good years can be greater than base salary. Carried interest is calculated in many ways, but basically it's the profit split of proceeds to the general partners. A ten-year industry veteran might make upward of $1 million. Oh, and if you discover the next Yahoo!, it would be considerably more. It's good to discover the next Yahoo!

The financial performance of investment banks tends to follow the market as a whole. Downturns mean smaller bonuses and possibly layoffs. Upturns tend to put you on the gravy train.

Consulting

For those who prefer PowerPoint to Excel, there is consulting. Consultants generally work in teams to solve problems or craft strategy for client companies. It's a tremendous job for people who aren't sure where they want to end up, since they can often "sample" different industries and functions. The job also offers great exposure to senior client executives—and making a good impression can mean a lucrative job offer down the line.

Consulting comes in just about every imaginable size and flavor. Big firms vs. boutiques, generalists vs. specialists, strategy vs. implementation. Each has its idiosyncrasies. While not every consultant spends five days a week on the road, you should be prepared for some travel. As an associate, you could spend a month in Austin helping a high-tech company launch a new product and two weeks later be in New York preparing a slide deck called "strategic insights" for a major consumer-goods producer. As you move up, you do more high-level synthesis and client relationship management.

Just out of business school, you can expect to make anywhere from $75,000 to $150,000 in the consulting industry. Typically, you start out as an associate or a consultant, and move up to engagement manager, principal, and finally, over six to ten years, partner. What do partners pull down? There's a huge, huge range, but here are a couple of numbers to put in your back pocket: At most shops, a partner makes well into the six figures (certainly over a half mil), and at top shops, like McKinsey, you could be looking at seven figures.

For the risk averse, consulting is relatively recession-proof. Companies need expertise in good times and in bad.

Marketing

If you have good "soft" skills and like brand issues (pricing strategies, new product development), you might be happy as a brand manager for a consumer-products company. Recent B-school grads might start out as an assistant marketing manager, eventually working their way up to a director- or VP-level position. Marketing managers develop, launch, and manage products as diverse as computers, web sites, butter substitutes, pet snacks, medical devices, pants, credit cards, and soda pop.

Starting salaries range from $75,000 to $100,000 for recent graduates. In marketing, the pay doesn't increase as rapidly as in other fields: Five years out, you could be looking at $150,000, and ten years out, between $200,000 and $300,000. Some say that generous perks—both from your employer and from vendors—can somewhat make up for lower paychecks. Hours, too, tend not to be as intense as in consulting or banking, although brand review periods are notoriously tough. Related fields like advertising and public relations also hire MBAs, though not as aggressively as "pure" marketers.

A Few Other Fields

If your goal is to attend the MTV Video Music Awards, dive into the **media & entertainment** scene. One option is to join the M&E practice at a big bank or consulting firm. But there are also opportunities for MBAs in business development, marketing, finance, and strategy for big media conglomerates like Disney, AOL Time-Warner, Bertelsmann, and Viacom. M&E salaries for recent grads aren't as high as their Big Three counterparts. Still, if you like the idea of rubbing elbows with the "in crowd" in New York or L.A., you might not mind the pay haircut. You're looking at a starting range of $70,000 to $100,000.

If you like the sound of "mogul," don't overlook a career in **real estate**. Project management for a developer involves organizing the construction process from site to sale. Real estate operations in investment banking, private equity, and commercial banking deal with the money that goes into funding property development, renovation, or purchases. Be prepared for long hours with few perks; B-schoolers who enter this field are strong in quant skills and don't mind putting in their time. Expect a starting salary in the range of $80,000 to $100,000.

If you're seeking risk and commensurate reward, **entrepreneurship** could be your cup of tea. Taking a job with a **start-**

up can still be a great learning opportunity for a freshly minted MBA. First it was e-commerce and wireless; now it's all about optical networking plays and interactive TV. But there are also furniture stores, T-shirt manufacturers, restaurants—the possibilities are endless and ever-changing, and the salaries depend on the particular company. The upsides include increased responsibility, nontraditional job titles, really cool office interiors, an average age peaking at thirty-five, and stock options that could net you a small fortune if you and your company deliver. The downside? Job insecurity and a less-structured work environment. But if you're looking to strike out on your own, it'll help you learn not to take a paycheck for granted.

Finely honed business skills are also much sought after at **nonprofits**. As in for-profit companies, you may find yourself working in finance, HR, strategic planning, marketing, or general management. And nonprofits are much more than the local art center: Greenpeace, the Red Cross, or the American Cancer Society all potentially hire MBAs.

Of course, this is just a taste of what's ahead. You'll find out a great deal more about each of these careers, and others, as you go forward. You'll hear from other students who have worked in these industries, you'll attend plenty of career presentations, and you will have the chance to test-drive an industry during your in-between summer.

WHAT WILL YOU BE STUDYING?

So what kind of "business" do they teach in business school anyway? Open the course catalog for any B-school, and you'll do one of two things: Either you will proceed directly to the section for the major you're interested in, or you'll be overwhelmed by the number and variety of classes, majors, and tracks available.

You will be required to choose a concentration for graduation, but don't worry, you won't have to decide right away. Since B-schoolers come from all walks of life, nearly all programs require first-years to take a group of core classes, designed to put everyone on a level playing field. They'll provide you with a basic grounding in the main areas of study, and you will be that much better prepared to focus on one (or more) for the remainder of your term. And remember: A B-school major doesn't lock you into a specific career; it's perfectly reasonable for a former consultant to round out her skill set by majoring in finance and then to go on to work for a high-tech start-up.

The most popular B-school concentrations are: management, finance, and marketing. Other oft-chosen majors include strategy, operations, public policy, real estate, insurance/risk management, and organizational behavior. Newer programs that are showing up in more and more schools' rosters include e-business management, entrepreneurship, technology/innovation, media/entertainment, and international business. Diehard number crunchers gravitate toward the ever-useful—if not always sexy—accounting, statistics, tax, or economics.

Keep in mind that most schools offer alternatives to the traditional major. So, for example, you may major in finance but have a concentration in a newer area, like entrepreneurship or media/entertainment. This allows you to focus on multiple areas. Some schools will let you minor in such fields as transportation, arts administration, environmental management, and legal studies.

Even within a major, some schools have subspecialties. So, for example, within a management major, you might focus on health-care administration, hotel administration, human resources administration, multinational business management, or industrial management. In short, you can go as broad or as specific as you want.

TOP MBA RECRUITERS

ABN AMRO Bank—investment banking

Accenture—consulting

American Express—financial services, marketing

American Management Systems—high-tech, consulting, new media

AMR Corp. (American Airlines)—marketing, finance

Arthur D. Little—consulting

A.T. Kearney—consulting

Bain & Co.—consulting

Bank of America Corporation—investment banking

Barclays Capital Group—investment banking

Bear Stearns & Co.—investment banking

Bertelsmann Inc.—media/entertainment, marketing

Booz-Allen & Hamilton—consulting

The Boston Consulting Group—consulting

Cap Gemini Ernst & Young—consulting

Charles Schwab & Co.—financial services

CIGNA—health care, finance, marketing

Citigroup—investment banking, financial services

Credit Suisse First Boston—investment banking

Dell Computer Corporation—high-tech, marketing

Deloitte Consulting—consulting

Deutsche Bank Alex. Brown—investment banking

Diamond Cluster International—high-tech, consulting

Dresdner Kleinwort Benson—investment banking

Eli Lilly and Company—marketing, finance

Enron Corp.—financial services, marketing

Ford Motor Co.—marketing

GE Capital/GE—high-tech, financial services, marketing

General Mills—marketing

General Motors—marketing, finance

Goldman Sachs—investment banking

Hewlett-Packard—high-tech, marketing

IBM—high-tech, marketing, finance, consulting

Intel—high-tech, marketing

J.P. Morgan Chase—investment banking

Johnson & Johnson—marketing

KPMG Consulting—consulting

Lehman Brothers—investment banking

LVMH Moet Hennessy Louis Vuitton—marketing

Marakon Associates—consulting

McKinsey & Co.—consulting

Mercer Management Consulting—consulting

Merrill Lynch—investment banking

Microsoft—high-tech, finance, marketing

Morgan Stanley Dean Witter—investment banking

Nomura Securities International—investment banking

Nortel Networks—high-tech

Pillsbury—marketing

PricewaterhouseCoopers—consulting

Procter & Gamble—marketing

Salomon Smith Barney—investment banking

SAP—high-tech, consulting

Sun Microsystems—high-tech, marketing

UBS Warburg—investment banking

United Technologies—high-tech, marketing, financial services

Wells Fargo—financial services

3

Choosing the Right School

THERE ARE 376 ACCREDITED BUSINESS SCHOOLS IN THE UNITED STATES AND DOZENS IN EUROPE, ASIA, AND OTHER PARTS OF THE WORLD. GIVEN ALL THE OPTIONS, WHICH SCHOOLS SHOULD YOU apply to? Which one is the perfect fit for you? And how do you decide?

A good place to start is a map. Where do you want to be? Where don't you want to be? Once you figure that out, you have to consider how big a school you want to attend, what you want to study, and what you think you want to do after getting your degree. Is there a learning style that appeals to you? Do you get, well, a good vibe from a school's brochure? Are there people you like and respect who graduated from a particular school? Then there are the issues of *how* you're planning to attend: full- or part-time? Single or dual degree? And, of course, there are the rankings. (For a roundtable discussion about B-school ranking, see Appendix A.) Don't forget: The best-ranked school isn't necessarily the best for you.

Naturally, you'll want to think hard about all this. Generally speaking, a smart first move is to determine the range of schools you think you can get into, then prioritize that list based on variables like location and class size. Scholarship money and financial aid may become an additional part of the equation once you're accepted. But for now, break out the legal pad and start making lists.

PART-TIME VERSUS FULL-TIME:
HOW DO YOU TAKE YOUR MBA?

Take two years off from your life? Say goodbye to a great job? Give up a decent paycheck? Eat campus food? These are just four reasons the whole full-time student thing doesn't appeal to everyone. Which is why many schools offer part-time B-school programs that fit real-world schedules. In fact, 64 percent of all MBA students pursue their degree on a part-time basis (although many switch midway to full-time, according to the International Association for Management Education). This allows a student to retain his or her job—and paycheck—while pursuing a degree. A few of the issues to consider when making your decision:

Do You Plan to Stay in Your Current Field?   If you want to advance in your current career, there's no reason not to go the part-time route. Obviously, if you're inclined to stay in your current career, you don't want to miss out on two years of on-the-job learning and who knows how many opportunities to advance. (Not to mention all the juicy office gossip about Weird Stan, the office manager.) But if you're thinking about a career switch, full-time is your best bet. Why? B-schools often restrict part-timers from some of their recruiting services. They do this for two reasons: First, they already have jobs, and finding employment for full-time students is a school's top priority. Second, employers foot the bill for many part-time MBA candidates, and they don't want their employees poached by other recruiters. Thus, part-time students can find it difficult to meet with companies; they may be restricted to certain interview categories or have to meet recruiters outside of the set schedule. Being a part-time student and a full-time worker also means you won't have time for a summer internship; and if you want to break into a new field, employers will want to see experience on your resumé. Some students who start part-time end up quitting their jobs and taking a full load of classes in order to get the most out of their business school's career center.

The Money Thing.   Although business school is clearly a great investment, it's expensive. Really expensive. If you simply can not forgo your paycheck, part-time is a way to make it happen. In addition to not losing your salary, many employers reimburse part or all of your tuition bills, so this can be a double win.

Your Work Schedule.   If your job demands that you log sixty to eighty hours a week in the office, you won't be able to add another fifteen to twenty of class time and homework to that without busting a vein. Trying to squeeze B-school into an already hectic schedule will prove frustrating for three reasons: (1) you'll feel like you're not able to give your all to either area, (2) you'll feel like you're not succeeding in either area, and (3) you won't have five damn minutes to yourself. If your work schedule is insane, quit your job and go to school full-time.

The Humanity of Your Boss.   Will your boss and your colleagues support your decision? You'll need some level of accommodation in order to make your schedule work; if your boss is not willing to support this and if your colleagues will resent the special treatment, you'll have an extremely difficult time.

Part-Timers Don't Get Equal Treatment.   A business school education is more than simply learning the skills of finance, marketing, and management. It's an experience. Going full-time allows more opportunities to network with professors, to brainstorm (or play poker) with other students, to listen to afternoon speakers, and to join special-interest clubs. As a part-timer, you'll miss out on much of this. So before you commit either way, think about how important these extracurriculars are to you.

Beyond that, part-timing it can make you feel like a second-class citizen at times. As mentioned, recruiting privileges are not always dispensed equally. Preference is sometimes given to full-timers for class space, and many courses are only offered during the day, when part-timers are working. Also, professors tend to have their office hours during the day.

And in the Final Analysis.   Of course, once you hit the real world, there is little or no difference between the two degrees: You went to the same school and took the same classes. Part timers will have done it while holding down a full-time job. Unlike their full-time classmates, they are able to apply knowledge in real time: learn something on Tuesday, put it to work on Wednesday. And the part-time peers at school may be very helpful in terms of providing contacts at their firms. It will take a bit longer to reach the prize—three or four years instead of two—but you *will* get there. Graduating with a part-time degree means you're that much further along in your career—and that much better off financially. In the end, as a part-timer you may even be afforded an extra measure of respect for your efforts: It's not everyone who can juggle such huge responsibilities.

THE DUAL DEGREE—TWO-FOR-ONE SPECIAL

Call her wacky/zany/nutty/crazy, but Terri McBride gets her kicks examining currency exchange rates, foreign debt transactions, and International Monetary Fund policies. With this

by Mark Murray

SEVEN TIPS TO MAKE
PART-TIME WORK FOR YOU

1. **Forget your undergrad study habits.** You won't have time during the week for homework. And you definitely won't have time to procrastinate or "study" over a few beers. You'll have to block out hours on the weekend— maybe the entire weekend, if need be.

2. **Stay on target.** Once you've enrolled, make B-school your priority. The business world moves at a rapid clip— you don't want to drag out your education for so long that your education becomes obsolete.

3. **Find another part-timer to watch your back.** Definitely make friends in your program. Fellow part-timers know what you're going through. You can study together and catch each other up on stuff if you have to miss a class.

4. **Investigate options.** Many part-timers find their situation has changed after a year or two and switch into the full-time program for the remainder of their degree. This may be a good option for you, so keep it in mind for down the road.

5. **Work it.** Even if you don't have the time to schmooze like a full-time student, join a club or two just to get on the mailing lists for career-boosting events. Go to speaker series or other events whenever feasible.

6. **Telecommute.** If your boss is amenable, save an hour or two every day by cutting down on time spent in traffic or riding mass transit.

7. **Take a break.** Yes, you will often feel over your head in demands and homework. But if you don't use your vacation days, you'll be on the fast track to burnout city.

by Sheila Resari

passion for global economics, it made sense for McBride to take advantage of one of the nation's most prestigious joint-degree graduate programs, which allows her to simultaneously get an MBA from the University of Pennsylvania's Wharton School and a master's degree from Johns Hopkins's Paul H. Nitze School of Advanced International Studies (SAIS).

McBride is a firm believer that two is better than one when it comes to higher education. While the MBA program fine-tunes her understanding of the international business world, the Johns Hopkins course work broadens her understanding of the history and economic systems of foreign countries. Even before finishing, she had already won offers from the State Department, the Treasury Department, and a top-notch New York management-consulting firm. "It's easy to understand the benefits of going to the number one business school," she says, "but I think the SAIS degree pays off in the long term."

Although only a small portion of the B-school population (estimates hover between 5 and 10 percent) enrolls in dual-degree programs, there are those, like McBride, who have chosen to dance the graduate-degree two-step. And the numbers are climbing. Schools across the country are making the joint degree easier than ever by combining programs that attract students with all types of interests. Those pursuing MBAs, for example, can get additional degrees in law, medicine, dentistry, public health, public policy, social work, computer science, and even animal husbandry.

Again, the overwhelming majority take their MBA straight, no chaser. But depending on your career goals, there are some potential pluses to pursuing a two-in-one deal:

Specialization

If you know exactly what you want to do, earning a complementary degree can help focus your studies and later your job search. "An MBA is just not enough for those who want to pursue something off the beaten path," claims Rose Martinelli, Wharton's director of MBA admissions and financial aid. "An MBA gives a lot of foundation, but it doesn't always give you the specialization that you might want to have."

Flexibility

For people like Scott Sherman, a dual degree provides an alternate set of skills. For almost as long as he can remember, Sherman wanted to be a lawyer. Yet, after two years at Columbia Law School and two summers interning as an associate at a couple of New York law firms, he was having doubts about his calling. So he decided to take advantage of Columbia's MBA-JD program to obtain the business skills that he missed as a pre-law undergrad at Duke University.

Most joint programs require that you apply for each degree individually—and be accepted to both independently. Students commonly do what Scott Sherman did and apply to a second program once they've already completed much of the first. In fact, McBride completed a year at SAIS before she applied for the dual degree at Wharton.

More Bang for Your Buck

Obtaining a dual degree is also considerably cheaper than pursuing two degrees separately. A Wharton MBA, (living, books, and all) for instance, costs about $100,000, and at SAIS, the degree costs about $70,000. You can combine them, however, for the low, low price of $120,000. Of course, this sum is nothing to sneeze at, but neither is saving $50,000 by pursuing both degrees simultaneously. A joint program also shaves months, or even up to a year, off the time it would take to earn the degrees separately.

Expense

Pursue a joint degree only if you're confident that your value as a job candidate will increase. Taking on a duffel bag full of debt to pay for a degree that you're not going to use is a bad investment.

Lack of Focus

In addition, for some postgraduate jobs, employers can be skeptical of students from joint programs, because two degrees can sometimes signal a lack of focus. "I tell everyone to be cautious," says Peter Veruki, the executive director of admissions and career planning at Rice University's Jones Graduate School of Business. "I've seen cases where it closes more doors than it opens." Veruki recounts one story of a student whose MBA-JD was perceived as a hindrance by a brand-management company during the interviewing process: "All that they wanted was an MBA who was hungry to do brand management."

Paul McLoughlin, president of the McLoughlin Company, an executive search firm based in New York, has this advice for students thinking of participating in a joint program: Have a good story to explain to interviewers why you've pursued two degrees. "I think the joint-degree program works when individuals . . . know what they are going to use them for."

If you do decide to take the dual-degree plunge, consider this advice from seasoned veterans:

When you combine an MBA with another master's program such as public policy or public health, be smart about dividing the curriculum, particularly if you want to take advantage of classmate networking. Many three-year joint programs within the same school require you to take one discipline in the first year, the other in the second, and both in the third. Dual programs at different institutions may require students to finish one degree before starting the next. Some say that taking the MBA component the first year is a mistake, because by the time you return to the business school for your third year, your original business classmates will already have graduated. All of your friends and all the contacts you're making are going to be gone. One of the most important things you get out of business school is the networking.

PAYING FOR THE MBA

Okay, so you've found the school that's a perfect fit—and you're confident you can get in. After tuition, books, and living expenses, one year at many U.S. business schools can cost $45,000. You have precisely $2,122.82 in the bank and are giving up your full-time job to attend. Your parents have offered moral support—but that's about it. So how to pay for it?

Scholarships, grants, and part-time work are all options to help finance the MBA. Most students tend to seek loans, but there are a tremendous number of scholarship opportunities overlooked every year.

Loans. This is the easiest approach, and most students seek loans because they are banking on a decent salary to kick in after graduation that will help pay them off. Loans come from three major sources: schools, private lending companies, and the federal government.

Schools will probably offer money more freely and with fewer contingencies than private institutions or the federal government. So once you've targeted the school choice, find out about the borrowing options there. Federal loans (Federal Stafford or Federal Direct Loans) are generally flexible about giving approval even if you have preexisting debt (but you cannot be in default on any other federal loans). The limit on federal loans is $18,500 per year. Federal loans usually boast lower interest rates than private lenders. Private institutions, however, can lend a greater amount. To get credit from a bank or other lending institution, it's best to pay off all debts and credit cards before applying for private loans. It will increase your chances of approval, reduce the rates, and provide better peace of mind. The Access Group is a private organization that lends funds up to the cost of attendance, and the rate is reasonable: short-term Treasury bill rate plus 3 points. The Graduate Management Admission Council (GMAC)—which administers the GMAT (Graduate Management Admission Test)—also has loan programs.

There is a small bit of consolation for those piling up debt to pay for the MBA: Some bigger firms are willing to pay for your schooling once you have accepted an offer. This is definitely something to ask about when you are mulling over your offers.

If just the thought of debt brings on an anxiety attack, there are other options.

Scholarships.   Many schools offer need-blind merit scholarships, ranging from $1,000 to $2,000 per year to a full ride. Some admissions committees dole out scholarships after reviewing applications, while other programs require separate essays before they grant money to incoming students. Check out fastweb.com for access to an extensive list of scholarships and application rules and deadlines. There is also Sallie Mae's Online Scholarship Program, the College Board's Fund Finder scholarship database, and also findaid.org (go to Scholarships). Most important, inquire at each school you apply to about what the opportunities are. Most have a special information packet or the like on the topic. Investigate which categories you qualify for—and go for it. With a relatively small degree of effort, most students can get something to help pay their tuition, so it's definitely worth making the effort. Similar to the application process itself, the earlier you apply, the better positioned you will be to get the good stuff.

Jobs.   For those willing to part with precious study time, there are ample opportunities to temp, intern, or become a teaching assistant. Assisting a prof is generally not that taxing and pays pretty well. Career offices can be a great help with finding and getting internships and part-time jobs, which can also establish great connections as you look for that full-time gig once school's out.

Finally, a note on the cost of the money. Many times, applicants are accepted at multiple schools, with a great degree of variation in the scholarship component. This can present a dilemma if your top-choice school is not as forthcoming with the green as other programs. What should you do if this is the case with you? First, try to select the school you think is the best for you, regardless of the money issue. If the difference between that program and the higher-paying school is less than $5,000 per year, choose your top pick, and don't even think twice. Do likewise if your other option, the better-paying one, is far down the rankings list (10 to 15 spots or more). If your options are close in rank and far apart in scholarship dollars, you may want to consider the one offering you the package, depending on what kind of hardship not getting the money represents. It is also fair to tell the school in question that it is your first choice but that financial considerations are keeping you from accepting. An admissions professional might be able to identify scholarship options you missed. You might also want to solicit the advice of recent alums for this potentially tough decision.

B-SCHOOL COMPARISONS

A lot goes into selecting the school that's right for you. Yes, yes, the rankings. But what about other important factors, such as . . . how long it takes for pizza to be delivered to campus or how late the computer help-desk is open? Below are some tables that show how a selection of schools stack up.

Closing Ceremonies
Sizing Up the Festivities on Graduation Day

	Yale	Arizona St.	Penn St.	Tulane	McGill	UNC
2001 Class Size	210	205	112	91	180	273
Commencement speaker	Thomas Krens, director of the Guggenheim Museum, NYC	Roy Vallee, chairman and CEO of Avnet	Jerry Sandusky, former Penn State football defensive coach	Tom Sams, 01, president of Tulane Graduate Business Council	Harvey Cox, professor at Harvard Divinity School	Fred Smith, chairman and CEO of FedEx
Exciting graduation tradition	MBAs announce the next student to receive diploma	Alumni toss cigars at new graduates	Catered barbecue on last day of class	Party with jambalaya and New Orleans funk music	Formal dinner and dance	Pig roast on a farm with clowns
Number of hours spent in classroom over two years	780	960	600	868	800	1,024
Percent of MBAs graduating with jobs	92	81	84	91	94	98
What students won't miss about B-school	"8.30 a.m. classes"	"Balancing multiple learning teams"	"All-nighters. With learning teams"	"Excel"	"Winters in Montreal"	"Company presentations"

Home Field Advantage
Eight B-Schools Compare Stats on the Sporting Life

	Harvard	Stanford	Ohio State	USC	University of Michigan	Wharton	Fuqua	Kellogg
Swimming pool lanes	14	38	27	18	17	17	12	17
Maximum # of simultaneous basketball courts	2	8	26	4	7	6	11	7
Stairmasters per 1,000 students	3.9	2.3	0.2	0.9	1.4	1.8	2.2	2.3
Tennis courts	4	26	12	12	16	14	14	18
Intramural sports offered university-wide	6	23	10	22	45	14	14	13
Bowling lanes within 10-minute drive of campus	118	72	118	95	120	82	72	44

Hooking Up
Who's Got the Best Connections? A Look at B-Schools in the Information Age

	Berkeley	Carnegie Mellon	Thunderbird	Columbia	Darden	Kellogg	Pepperdine
Percentage of classrooms wired	62	100	7	85	100	53	100
Number of e-business courses	29	13	9	7	7	16	4
Campus tech support hours	7:30 a.m.- 10 p.m.	7 a.m. - 10 p.m.	8 a.m. - 5 p.m.	8 a.m. - 8 p.m.	7:30 a.m. - 5:30 p.m.	8:30 a.m. - 8 p.m.	6 a.m. - midnight
Cost to send one page from campus fax	$2.00	Free	$1.00	$1.00	Free	50¢	Free
Number of cell-phone stores in phone book	9	5	10	4	4	6	0
Two hours online at nearby net cafe	$20.00	None in area	$8.00	$26.00	Free	$19.00	$3.00

At Your Service
Eight Campuses Go Head-to-Head on Every Modern Convenience

	Harvard	NYU	University of Kansas	UT– Austin	Michigan State	University of Chicago	University of Washington	UCLA
# of feet from main building to closest FedEx drop-off	1,425	610	0	45	1,689	743	1,109	0
Prices per pound of wash-dry-fold at local laundromat	75¢	70¢	75¢	$1.25	95¢	$1.00	$1.00	$1.10
Cost of weekly cleaning service for 1br. apartment	$95.00	$45.00	$50.00	$60.00	$45.00	$55.00	$50.00	$50.00
Minutes delivery time for closest non-Domino's pizza	30	15	40	30	30	45	30	45
Plumbers, locksmiths who advertise 24-hour services	40	63	14	43	34	66	41	45
Computer help services in local phone book	193	186	7	128	56	112	150	69

Master Plans
Business-Plan Contests Go Under the Lights

	University of Washington	USC	Insead/ London Business School	North-eastern	Fuqua	University of Chicago	Ivey School University of Western Ontario
Number of entries	41	20	11	133	57	105	50
First-place prize	$25,000	A silver cup	$3,000	$40,000	$30,000	$20,000	$10,000
Perks for winner	Incubator space	None	Management consulting and legal services	Accounting and legal services	None	Web-marketing services, legal services	Trip to Australia for international competition
Number of judges	132	5	5	7	8	15	20
Last year's winning company	Aptelix, cell-phone e-mail soft-ware	Channel IP, brokers excess satellite transmission	iFox, over-the-counter derivatives exchange	LoanBright, mortgage broker web site	OmnipreSense, human-computer interface devices	Implantable micro devices	Dementiaguide. com, software for Alzheimer's patients and doctors

CATEGORY LEADERS

Here's a quick look at some of the top programs for specific fields of interest.

Best for Technology

MIT (Sloan), Carnegie Mellon, Pennsylvania (Wharton), Northwestern (Kellogg), Stanford, Harvard, Chicago, Cornell (Johnson), Duke (Fuqua), Virginia (Darden)
(SOURCE: *Business Week*)

Best Student-Faculty Ratios

Purdue, Indiana (Kelley), Georgia Tech (DuPree), Michigan State (Broad), INSEAD, UNC–Chapel Hill (Flagler), Duke (Fuqua), UT–Austin (McCombs), Carnegie Mellon, Stanford, Virginia (Darden)
(SOURCE: *Business Week*)

Best in Global Business

London Business School, Pennsylvania (Wharton), Columbia, Harvard, NYU (Stern), Michigan–Ann Arbor, Stanford, Thunderbird, South Carolina (Moore), Washington U. (Olin), UNC–Chapel Hill (Flagler)

(SOURCE: *Financial Times, Business Week*)

Best in Nonprofit Management

Yale, Harvard, Northwestern (Kellogg), Stanford, Case Western (Weatherhead), Columbia, Pennsylvania (Wharton), Cornell (Johnson), Thunderbird, Suffolk U. (Sawyer)

(SOURCE: *U.S. News, Business Week*)

Best Part-Time Programs

NYU (Stern), Chicago, Northwestern (Kellogg), UCLA (Anderson), DePaul (Kellstadt), Michigan–Ann Arbor, USC (Marshall), UC–Berkeley (Haas), Georgia State (Robinson), Babson

(SOURCE: *U.S. News*)

Top Programs for E-Commerce

MIT (Sloan), Carnegie Mellon, Pennsylvania (Wharton), Western Ontario, Stanford, Northwestern (Kellogg), UT–Austin (McCombs), UC–Davis

(Source: SOURCE: *Business 2.0, Business Week*)

Great Schools for Women

NYU (Stern), Chicago, Michigan, UC–Berkeley (Haas), Stanford, Northwestern (Kellogg), Virginia (Darden), Rotterdam

(SOURCE: *Working Woman*)

Great Schools for Entrepreneurs

Babson (Olin), UCLA (Anderson), Berkeley (Haas), IMD (Switzerland), USC (Marshall), Stanford, Maryland (Smith), UT–Austin (McCombs), Rice (Jones), SMU
(SOURCE: *Financial Times*)

Strong Finance Programs

Pennsylvania (Wharton), Chicago, Harvard, Columbia, Northwestern (Kellogg), Duke (Fuqua), Michigan, INSEAD, MIT (Sloan), NYU (Stern), Virginia (Darden)
(SOURCE: *Financial Times*)

Strong Marketing Programs

Northwestern (Kellogg), Pennsylvania (Wharton), Harvard, Duke (Fuqua), Michigan, Virginia (Darden), Columbia, IESE (Spain), Cornell (Johnson), Chicago, Stanford
(SOURCE: *Business Week*)

Strong in General Management

Northwestern (Kellogg), Harvard, Michigan, Pennsylvania (Wharton), Virginia (Darden), INSEAD, Duke (Fuqua), Stanford, Chicago, Columbia, Cornell (Johnson)
(Source: SOURCE: *Business Week*)

AN INTERNATIONAL PERSPECTIVE

Kai Peters, dean at the Rotterdam School of Management in the Netherlands, makes the case for spreading out the map, renewing your passport, and getting your degree abroad.

You're thinking of attending B-school in another country—maybe just to broaden your universe, possibly to build contacts if you decide to work abroad after school. What are the options? How is it a different experience? Is it a good career move? Kai Peters has thought extensively about those very subjects. The forty-year-old program awards graduate business degrees to 120 students from fifty-two countries. In his ten years with the program, Peters has helped position the Rotterdam School among the top programs in Europe—indeed the world, coming in at number twenty-nine on the *Financial Times* 2001 world B-school rankings. Dean Peters discussed with *Jungle* his thoughts on the globalization of the business-school community, the increasing intensity of corporate recruiting, the different B-school philosophies around the world, and the need for an adventurous spirit.

Do you think that an American who wants to work in Europe can get a leg up in his job search by going to a European business school?

Absolutely. If you have your heart set on working in Europe, you can really benefit by spending a year or a year and a half in your country of choice. You will have better access to the recruiters, and you will be able to develop your own European networks.

We have two types of North American students at Rotterdam. We have the people who come for the whole MBA, but we also have a good number of exchange students who will have gone to one of the partner schools with whom we work in the states—Wharton, Kellogg, Chicago, and others. They'll come for a semester. Many of the exchange students end up working in Europe afterward.

Suppose you have an American student who's accepted into, say, Chicago and Rotterdam. Why should he go to Rotterdam?

Well, let's presume this person has a good undergraduate degree, he's grown up near New York City, he understands how business is conducted, he has networks and contacts, and he understands the landscape in the U.S. To differentiate themselves from the other candidates, they should strongly consider an expertise that can be developed by being in another market: you're going to learn other business styles, you're going to learn about the geography. Just being in Europe for a year or a year and a half provides a different impression, a different perspective on the world. When companies look at this person's resumé this diversity of background will really pop out.

Are you seeing an increasing number of Americans going to European schools?

We've had a number of engineers from places like Cornell, who were twenty-eight and who wore Timberlands and shorts and plaid shirts. They were told by investment banks: "Look. Your grades are good, you got a wonderful GMAT score, but you really are quite similar to a lot of the East Coast MBA crowd. Why don't you go to Rotterdam or to London and do something different? When you come back you're going to have an added set of values that you're bringing to us."

Why else should someone consider going to B-school abroad?

Business schools in the states have such a high cost, plus living, which is not cheap either. So you have to think about your net present value calculation on your business school experience. If you come to any of the European schools you're gonna get out of there with a lower debt load and with a higher sense of adventure. Then it's up to you what career you want to pursue. If you want to go for the high-end experience—well-paid consulting or I-banking in New York—you can do that. But you can also say, "I want to work in marketing" or "I want to work in Europe for another year" or "I'm willing to go to China for a year because I know I'm not a victim of a mortgage on my life."

Do you see any kind of major difference in the way programs are outlined or the way courses are taught in Europe, Asia, and the U.S.?

In North America I would say that 95 percent of the programs are university-based business schools. There is much greater diversity in Asia and in Europe, where you have INSEAD [a top school with campuses in France and Singapore] and IMD [the International Institute for Management, in Switzerland], which come from kind of a Chamber of Commerce consortium of companies that back them. There are a bunch that are university based, such as Rotterdam. And there are also the hybrids. They tend to have much greater diversity. In Europe, you have everything from ten-month programs to twenty-three-month programs and you have everything from a strong emphasis on case teaching to a strong emphasis on lecturing. There are also various regional differences in attitude and philosophy. For instance, the Scandinavians always say, "Well, everyone must be happy first and make money second." In the UK they say, "Well, let's make money first and think about being happy afterward."

Describe the corporate recruiting experience at Rotterdam in particlar and in Europe in general.

This past year we had 130 companies on campus—quite a few for 120 graduating students. In our case it's I-banks, consultants—surprise, surprise—and lots of tech companies, which I hope will continue because we've always had a solid technological focus. The Nokias, Ericssons, and Lucents all come and recruit. We have a lot of American companies that target European schools in order to expand their European business. That brings us companies like Enron, Reliant, Ford, and some of the banks.

WOMEN ON THE VERGE

Where Are the Women?

A fabulous education, great networking opportunities, a $127,000 starting salary, and a male-female ratio of three to one—with perks like these, women should be racing to business school. But women aren't buying it. Law and medical schools, even engineering programs, are seeing a rise in female students. But the number of women in MBA programs, while up significantly from the 1970s and 1980s, has lingered below 40 percent for nearly a decade.

To find out why, Catalyst, a nonprofit research organization devoted to promoting professional women, the University of Michigan's Business School, and its Center for the Education of Women joined forces to produce "Women and the MBA: Gateway to Opportunity," a seventy-four-page report that examines why the percentage of women seeking MBAs has remained static for so long.

"The biggest surprise was the incredible satisfaction level women reported," says Jeanne Wilt, assistant dean at Michigan and one of the lead writers of the report. Ninety-five percent were "somewhat satisfied." Catherine Jaccodine, Columbia '99, couldn't agree more. She gushes, "It is the best investment I have made to date."

Even more striking, only 27 percent of female MBAs thought business schools were overly competitive. Fully 20 percent of men did, too, so the difference in enrollment can't be attributed to this factor. These and other findings challenge the belief that women experience business school very differently than their male peers. Another example: Seventy percent of women say they experience no difficulty making discussion points during class. This number is lower than the 82 percent of men, but still quite high.

by Farah Miller

The catch, however, is that all the respondents were students who *had already been enrolled* in MBA programs. Why are so many women in business wary of B-school?

The Investment Banker Myth

It's no secret that women are not as encouraged to develop their quantitative skills. Forty-five percent of respondents in the Catalyst/University of Michigan study cited lack of confidence in mathematical ability as a reason that women do not pursue an MBA. Add to that the many women who imagine business school classrooms to be wall-to-wall investment bankers, and the result is that many prospective female MBAs, fearful of alpha-male quant jocks, are reluctant to enter the fray. This is a perception that many women, once enrolled, realize is simply not true. A recent mbajungle.com survey asked respondents to select what they thought the main cause is for low female enrollment in B-schools. The results: family/parenthood-related issues: 41 percent; math phobia: 19 percent; lack of mentors: 18 percent; alpha-male culture: 1 percent; other: 22 percent.

Family Time

Balancing life and work is an issue everyone can relate to, but it particularly stings women who want to get on the business world's fast track. "They wonder, if you're working seventy hours per week, what else do you have time to do?" explains Michigan's Wilt. The job experience usually necessary for potential MBAs can coincide almost directly with the years many female candidates choose for child rearing.

Some schools are hoping to attract more women by looking at readiness as opposed to the number of years worked. Other schools are hoping to lower the average age of B-schoolers (the average age today is twenty-eight), but this raises the question of whether the policy will insult women who want to be held to the same standard as men. Catalyst argues that to combat this issue, businesses and schools should work together to establish flexible workweeks for women with families. Also, Wilt points out that women who want to take a break for family should know an MBA will help when they are ready to return to work.

Entrepreneurship is another option for those who want more flexibility. Women don't need MBAs to get started, but Marianne Danko, Cornell's Johnson School '99, says, "A woman business owner without an MBA won't have the network I got from business school." In spite of the more than 9 million women-owned businesses flourishing today, only about 4 percent of venture capital goes to female entrepreneurs. That number might rise if more women business owners were also MBAs, Danko surmises.

Role Models Are Missing

Fifty-six percent of Catalyst's respondents say a lack of female role models is why women aren't going to business school. In the corporate world, only 12.5 percent of Fortune 500 company board members are women. In business schools, only 11 percent of deans are women.

This is a trend many business leaders and schools are working to reverse. For example, the Committee of 200 is a nineteen-year-old group of women entrepreneurs and executives whose mission is to promote entrepreneurship and corporate leadership among women. Associate Dean Mary Miller says NYU Stern is taking on this issue by recruiting more female faculty at every level in the business school. Coincidentally, the school's female enrollment level has run counter to the norm. In 2001–2002, Stern's first-year class is 37-percent female. Other schools, like Michigan, Berkeley, and Columbia are trying to keep up by actively recruiting women, too.

A Business School of Their Own

Perhaps nobody knows the value of a female community at business school better than Pat O'Brien, dean at Simmons Graduate School of Management, the only all-women MBA program. Simmons's faculty is 75-percent women, the majority of case studies are female-centric, and enrollment is climbing steadily. The program is seeking accreditation from AACSB, the generally accepted seal of approval. The school's class size has risen 25 percent in the last five years. "Here, no one is categorized as different because of gender," says O'Brien. "Sexual politics are gone. Our students go back to organizations more prepared to cope because we give them skills to work with men who manage differently."

Bottom Line

Although 95 percent of female MBAs express satisfaction with their business school experience, many of their peers still hesitate to apply, for reasons ranging from family concerns to a lack of role models.

The good news is they are hesitating less and less. When Simmons opened its doors twenty-eight years ago, only 7 percent of business school students were women. Today that number has increased sevenfold. Twenty-five years from now, this number will surely climb even further as B-school hallways become increasingly gender-balanced.

4

Getting In

·····················

HOW TO GET INTO TOP-CHOICE SCHOOLS

Gaze at these numbers: 8 percent, 12 percent, 14 percent. Those are the acceptance rates at Stanford, Columbia, and Wharton. If you're a prospective MBA student, you probably know them by heart. Obviously, getting into business school is difficult for even the most qualified applicants, and there is no magic formula that guarantees acceptance. Still, even the top schools have to admit someone, and it might as well be you.

So what does it take to stand out? In a word, *knowledge*. Specifically, self-knowledge. You need to think hard about why you want to get an MBA and what you plan to do with it—both immediately and five years after you graduate. And when you're done thinking about it, you need to be able to clearly and persuasively articulate it. To get in, you will need to be able to identify your strengths and weaknesses. Know the school you're applying to, how it can help you achieve your goals, and where you stand with regard to the rest of the applicant pool. Finally, know the process. Understanding how the admissions process works maximizes your chances of landing in the "accepted" pile.

---

by Robyn Gearey

WHERE TO APPLY: HOW TO PICK
THE RIGHT SCHOOL FOR YOU

The best schools for you are not necessarily the ones that *Business Week*, the *Financial Times*, or *U.S. News & World Report* rank first, second, and third. The top-tier schools have many advantages, of course—higher starting salaries, a more prestigious alumni network, and elite recruiters, among others. But even a top school may not satisfy other important criteria such as geographic location, specific areas of study, a particular professor, scheduling flexibility, cost, or a philosophy that meshes with your particular beliefs or learning style.

Not surprisingly, research is the key to determining which schools fit your needs. The best place to start is the Web: www.businessweek.com lets you look at all the schools in its survey, with detailed information from the survey as well as blurbs from current students. Embark's (www.embark.com) Matchmaker feature quizzes you on the importance of factors such as location, areas of study, selectivity, and placement information, then spits out a list of schools that match your criteria. And now for a shameless plug: mbajungle.com (specifically, the "Getting In" channel) lets you look at detailed profiles of every MBA program. You can also compare schools according to the specific criteria you establish and chat with other applicants and current students at each school.

It makes sense to calibrate which programs you think will accept you, and then apply to at least one school a few notches below. Also, apply to more than just two or three schools— each program is different, and even though the two schools may have a similar ranking, the assets you bring to the table may be more attractive to one school than another.

In any case, it pays to get to know the specific ins and outs of each school thoroughly. Admissions officials' single biggest gripe is the generic application—cookie-cutter essays and recommendations that don't speak to the individual school or the fit between the applicant and the school. For this level of detail, school web sites are the best resource.

INSIDER TIP. Most MBA programs have a school newspaper. Get at least one copy and read it. That will give you invaluable insights into the culture of the school, the personality of the place, the individuals within the school, and so on.

When to Apply

You'll notice that many schools have three or four application deadlines with drop-dead dates as late as March or April. That said, you would be—how to put this delicately?—a fool to actually apply this late in the game. Nearly every admissions director gives the same advice: Apply early. In the initial rounds, the field is clear and every space in the class is still open. That isn't likely to be the case a few months later. And as space tightens up, admissions officers can afford to be more choosy.

This is especially true at the most competitive schools, where the vast majority of the applicants are absurdly qualified. In a *Business Week* interview, the director of admissions at Dartmouth's Tuck School of Business Administration confessed that in 1999, just four people were admitted in the fourth round. And smart candidates know to apply early to Stanford, where the acceptance rate in the first round can be as high as 11 percent—better than the average acceptance rate of 8 percent. So just in case you were skimming this section, we'll say it again, and we'll say it loudly: APPLY EARLY.

Many schools encourage applicants to submit their applications electronically, either through the school's own web site or through a service such as embark.com or Multi-App (www.multi-app.com), which requires a fee to use the software

($12 to apply to a limited number of participating schools, $59 for unlimited access).

The Application

There is no formula for acceptance. Admissions directors will say this until they're blue in the face—which is quite fun to watch—and it's absolutely true. While policies vary from school to school, of course, business schools are very committed to evaluating the whole package that an applicant presents. Want proof? Chicago has accepted applicants with GMAT scores in the 300s; one year, Darden rejected five out of six applicants with perfect GMAT scores of 800. Wharton and other top schools have accepted students with less than two years' experience—and the experience came in a field other than business.

The examples above are clearly exceptions—most people getting into the top schools have some combination of strong grades, good GMAT scores, and valuable experience and have written excellent essays on why they want to attend and how they will make a good addition to the school.

Obviously, each applicant has his or her own strengths and weaknesses. The trick is to think about the picture that your application will present and try to balance out any weaknesses. For example, if you majored in philosophy or fine arts in college, make sure to prepare thoroughly for the quantitative part of the GMAT and consider taking a statistics, economics, or calculus course at a community college to prove you can handle the work. If your experience is in a nontraditional field such as teaching, journalism, or training albino hamsters to perform circus tricks, use your essays to highlight leadership roles that you've taken on and specific projects you've tackled. Making the admissions mindset your mindset will give you a distinct edge as you go through the application process.

INSIDER TIP. As you're preparing your application, it's extremely important to think about the person who will be reading it. And not just thinking about them, thinking *like* them. After talking with admissions officers at numerous top schools, three questions stand out as basic criteria:

- Will this person do well in our program? Translation: Will he or she stand up to the pressures, get good grades, get a lot out of what we do here? This is the part of the mindset that should be fairly intuitive.
- Will this person make a real contribution to the program? (Remember, you learn just as much from your peers as you do from your profs.) Translation: What does he or she bring to the table that others perhaps don't? Could be work experience that is extremely valuable to others. Could be a really outgoing personality that will make the environment better for all. Could be a propensity for leadership—maybe this person will get involved with student government or take the initiative/leadership reins at a club.
- Will this person be a good alum? Translation: Will he make us look good a few years down the road? If I were Goldman Sachs/Morgan Stanley/McKinsey & Co., would I hire this person? Will this alum be a leader someday? Will I read about this person in the newspaper and be proud she went to my school?

Under the Microscope: How Admissions Officers Look at Your Application

Undergraduate Grades. Your GPA is important (see "Key Admissions Data" at the end of this chapter), and schools are going to pay particular attention to your performance in quantitative courses such as calculus, statistics, accounting, and economics—especially if you majored in a nonquantitative field such as English or philosophy. The overall difficulty of your course load and the school's reputation will also be factored in.

Unless you're particularly skilled at breaking and entering, you can't go back and change your transcript. So what *can* you do to overcome a less-than-stellar college career? Strong GMATs and solid work experience might be enough, but your essays are powerful tools here. Use them to discuss circumstances that might have affected your GPA—perhaps you had to work your way through school, experienced a personal tragedy (steer clear of whining here, just talk about how the experience changed you), or were just young and too focused on having a great time instead of on academics. Whatever the reason, a well thought out essay discussing what you learned from the experience—and how you have put yourself on the right track since—can help your case immensely. Not addressing poor grades tends to raise question marks.

GMAT. Unlike the LSAT for law school, GMAT scores are rarely the sole determining factor for admission. But don't take them lightly. At top schools, you'll be competing against people with very high scores, so it pays to make sure that you can hold your own (see "Key Admissions Data" at the end of this chapter). Aim to land a GMAT score within fifty points of a school's average; if your score is lower, consider retaking the test. Schools don't generally notice or care how often you take the test—they only see the three most recent scores. However, unless there are extenuating circumstances, you aren't likely to raise your score dramatically from test to test, though prep courses can help a lot. (See the section on page 59 that deals specifically with the GMAT.)

Work Experience. In the 1980s, MBA students tended to have just two years of work experience or less. Today, applicants have often worked for at least four years, and many have even more experience than that. What admissions committees are looking for here is evidence that you've made progress in your career, taken on increasing responsibility, and demonstrated leadership in your company or field. Strong communications skills and a proven ability to work well in groups are also important. Highlight these experiences throughout your application.

Recommendations. This would seem to be the most straightforward part of the application, but in fact it trips up many, many candidates. Almost every school will want to see one recommendation from a current (or recent) supervisor. Choose your recommenders carefully—a letter from a well-known person won't help you as much as a thoughtful, positive letter from someone who really knows your work. The kiss of death is a poor recommendation. Who in his right mind would solicit a recommendation from someone who wouldn't rave? You'd be surprised. (Apparently we're not as good judges of how others see us as we think we are.) According to one admissions official at a top school, 10 percent of applicants include a recommendation in which the recommender is actually negative about the candidate. This alone will get your application on the express track to Rejectopolis. If you have any doubt whatsoever, ask the person directly if he feels comfortable writing a positive recommendation. If you get an ambiguous answer, say thank you and look elsewhere. By the same token, if the school gives you the option to provide an additional recommendation, think twice. Unless the recommender can really add something to your application, an additional letter can hurt more than it can help.

INSIDER TIP.   Admissions officers say that many recommendations lack personality and fail to make the applicant look unique. Instead, the person just checked off the boxes and made few personal comments. This lack of enthusiasm sends a strong message to the admissions committee. To help your recommendation stand out from the crowd, follow these steps:

- Make sure to give your recommenders enough time to do a thorough job.
- Give them a copy of your resumé, as well as a list of any other accomplishments. This will allow them easy access to your background and enable them to make specific references in their letter.
- Show them your application and brief them on how you believe you can best contribute to your particular school. The more informed they are about the school and your application as a whole, the better the recommendation will be.
- Giving them a nice bottle of wine for their time is a classy move that says you are a classy person.

The Essays

Let's start with three basics: Proofread! Proofread! And, oh, yes, proofread! You wouldn't believe the number of essays that top schools receive that contain typos or use the wrong school's name (an essay for the University of North Carolina's Flagler School, for example, discussing the writer's lifelong dream of attending Duke's Fuqua School of Business). Will a small mistake like this land an application in the reject pile? Maybe. Maybe not. But it sends a powerful message: The applicant is not detail-oriented and does not care to be. In short, it can color the way the admissions officers read the rest of the application. Make sure you have two other people carefully read your essays. Following directions is also crucial—schools do not appreciate essays that are over the word limit. If the directions say to double-space, then by all means double-space.

Admissions officers are also annoyed by the generic essay that doesn't really answer the particular question asked but just kinda sorta skirts the edges. Don't reuse or "tweak" the essay you wrote for one school for another school's application—admissions personnel can smell a "retrofit" from two miles away. Instead, take the time to make sure that the essay serves a purpose. It should highlight something about you that the rest of your application doesn't show. Anecdotal information is the most effective—be careful not to fall back on simply regurgitating your resumé. Essays that address a failure and demonstrate how you overcame it or show leadership can be extremely effective. But pick your topic carefully: Not making the soccer team in high school is, well, kind of lame. The gripping story of how you got to be vice president of your college sorority is perhaps even lamer. (Note: Do not use the word "lamer" anywhere in your essay.)

Wherever possible, use the essays to differentiate yourself from the other 3,000 applicants. One Wharton hopeful went so far as to include with her application a product she had invented. It worked: She got in, and two years later, the admissions office still remembered her application. But make sure to check with the school in question before you take such extreme measures—some admissions offices have strict policies against sending any additional material and will just toss your offering straight into the Dumpster.

INSIDER TIP. When describing how they overcame obstacles, many applicants have a tendency to describe all of their hard work. Instead of going on about how hard you worked, show how clever you were. Show how you grew from the experience and were able to apply it going forward. This is much more interesting than essays of the "working-on-the-railroad" variety, even if you were working really, really hard on the railroad.

It's important to understand what the school is looking for and to be able to articulate why you want to attend that particular program. Wherever possible, draw parallels between who you are and what you've done and the characteristic values of the school. There are also certain parts of the application—the essay is one of them—that invite you to step out of the square box and let your individuality show. Take advantage of this—and don't be afraid to let your personality shine through. In the end, that is what will make your application memorable.

The Interview

After you've sent your applications, you may be asked to come in for an interview. (Or you might request one—be sure to research each school's policy.) Some schools conduct interviews by invitation only, some will let anyone who wishes schedule an interview, and some don't interview at all. At invitation-only schools, it's generally a good sign if you are asked to interview, but again, know the school's policy. Some schools interview all candidates who are under serious consideration, while others use the interview to make a call on a borderline application.

Your interview might be on campus, or with an alum or campus representative in your area. In either case, unless you're told otherwise, dress professionally and treat it as you would a job interview: arrive promptly, don't talk negatively about your boss or your coworkers, and make sure that you are prepared to talk about why you want an MBA, why that particular school is the one you want to attend, and what you have to offer. You may also be asked what you see yourself doing five to ten years in the future.

The Decision

What should you do if you're wait-listed? Be patient and don't flood the admissions office with pleas from your Grandma

> **INSIDER TIP.** The interview is your chance to address your weak points or to bring one of your strong points to life. If you know you have a weakness, be ready to talk about it! Practice actually saying the answer to the question you know you will get, such as why your undergraduate GPA was on the low side. If you don't get asked such a direct question, listen carefully. The interviewer may be trying to ask you in an oblique manner. Don't fail to pick up on it. On the other hand, come prepared with at least one meaningful story on the positive side—one that they have not already read about on your application. It will show them that the application, and even this interview, are only scratching the surface of the amazing person/student/business genius you are, and will get them excited about having you join their team.

Minnie and Cousin Sue about why you should be admitted. (This does happen.) It's okay, however, to follow up with any supporting material that adds something new to your candidacy—maybe you got a promotion at work, or you retook the GMAT and received a higher score. Other levers: If you haven't had an interview (at an interview-optional school), request one. If you know a current student or alum at the school in question, ask the person to write a short (one page max) letter on your behalf to the admissions committee. The letter should clearly state that the writer knows the candidate is on the waiting list and then quickly spell out the reasons, from his perspective, that the candidate would be a great get for the school. It doesn't hurt for your supporter to add that their school is the candidate's first choice—admissions counselors want high accepted-offer rates, especially at a late stage in the game.

In this situation, it's also okay to ask the school for guidance; many will recommend something specific—take the GMAT again, get more work experience, cut your hair—and give you an idea of when you can expect an answer. (With the vast majority of schools, there's no predetermined date when candidates on the waiting list are notified one way or the other.) Finally, be aware of an option that several schools offer: deferred admission. Basically, this guarantees you a spot in the class for the following year.

If you didn't get in, don't beat yourself up. Many people who were not accepted the first time they applied were given the nod the following year, and now have an MBA to show for their perseverance. Approach the setback as you would starting a business: Think strategically. Think through your application to see where the weaknesses are and spend the next year addressing them. You should definitely seek feedback from the admissions committee on the gaps in your profile. If you ask for this information in an earnest, constructive manner—these people get lots of calls from angry people who want to blow off steam—you will usually get constructive feedback in return. They may tell you, for instance, that your GMAT score is holding you back. If that's the case, they may suggest that taking (and acing) a calculus class will help. Or perhaps they felt that you didn't have enough work experience, and another year in the trenches will get you where you need to be. In any event, you should definitely take advantage of this and follow their recommendations. You can then reapply the next year and have a much better chance of admission—at that school and others.

Reapplying to the same school is a bit of a double-edged sword, however: The committee at the school has already seen your "warts" but can also track the improvement from one year to the next. As many determined MBAs can attest, if there's real improvement, there's no reason you can't be admitted the second time around. On the other hand, in some cases you may be viewed through the lens of someone who has already rejected you. There's no way to know for certain, so on top of accepting all the constructive feedback and acting on it, definitely add a couple of new schools to your list for next year.

UNDERSTANDING THE GMAT

What Is the GMAT?

Well, officially, the Graduate Management Admission Test is a three-and-a-half-hour exam designed to measure your verbal and quantitative skills. The verbal section of the exam consists of reading comprehension, grammar, and logic questions, while the math section tests basic algebra, geometry, and arithmetic. The Analytical Writing Assessment consists of two thirty-minute essays. Overall, the test is designed to predict your academic performance in the first year of business school, and even more ambitiously, your future success in the world of business.

Now, not so officially: Although the GMAT theoretically tests your ability to do well in business school, some say all it tests is your ability to do well on the GMAT. But regardless of whether it's a good predictor of either academic ability or future success in business, it is used as an important metric in business school admissions. Further, many top firms—McKinsey and Goldman Sachs, for instance—routinely check GMAT scores as a part of their employment recruiting process. Like all standardized tests, the GMAT is a uniform tool for comparing students whose academic and professional backgrounds vary wildly.

The GMAT CAT

Since October 1, 1997, the GMAT has been offered in a computer-only format, known as the GMAT Computer Adaptive Test, or the GMAT CAT. Unlike a paper test, the CAT adapts to your performance as you proceed through the test. In fact, every person gets a different test depending on how well he or she is doing. Your final score is based not only

by Alicia Abell

on how many questions you get right but also on the difficulty level of the questions you answer correctly.

The test starts with a medium-level question. If you answer it correctly, you generally get a harder question; if you get it wrong, you usually get an easier question. This process continues throughout the test. Two test takers can get the same number of questions right but have very different scores. Here's how it works:

Total scores on the CAT range from 200 to 800. The answer to each question determines the degree of difficulty of the following question. Since tougher questions are worth more, you can take yourself out of the top range of scoring rather quickly. In general, the further you get into the test, the more you're just fine-tuning your score. And if you get a long string (say, five or six) wrong, you may get "easy" questions for the rest of the exam—on the CAT, that's bad, bad news.

> **INSIDER TIP.** Don't guess randomly at more than two questions in a row because strings of wrong answers can dramatically affect your score. The only exception to this is toward the end of the test—if you are running out of time, you will have to guess to complete the exam, but you should try to eliminate at least one wrong answer before guessing.

How Do CAT Scores Compare to Pencil and Paper?

As confusing as all this may sound, your score on the CAT is likely to be very similar to what it would be on the pencil-and-paper version of the test. Before switching over to the CAT, ETS (Educational Testing Service), which prepares the test, pretested and normed it to make sure the scores were comparable.

There are definite advantages to the CAT. Instead of scheduling your life around a predetermined date, you can sign up to take the test whenever is convenient for you. And, unlike with the pencil-and-paper version, you can see your scores immediately after completing the test. Finally, many people prefer to type their essays. This is obviously a huge benefit to people with sloppy, difficult-to-read handwriting. (Or "chicken scratchings," as it's known in professional circles.) "I loved the computer version when it came time for the essay portion," said one B-school candidate who took the CAT when ETS was pretesting it. "I type probably six times as fast as I write, so that helped a lot. I liked being able to cut and paste and make clean edits."

Of course, there are some downsides to the computerized GMAT. Not being able to go back to a question is the main one. The experimental questions also seem to unnerve students more on the CAT than on the paper-and-pencil version. On the CAT, "if you think you got a problem right, you're anticipating a harder one," explains a prospective student, who is currently studying for the exam. "You might have gotten a hard one right, and then you get an easy experimental question. And then you think you might have gotten the last question wrong. Psychologically, that's tough."

Finally, you have to use separate scratch paper when taking the CAT. "You have to take the crucial information from the screen that you need and transfer that to the paper," says one student. "For example, in reading comprehension, you can't circle key words." Plus, you have to scroll through the reading comprehension passages because you can't see the whole thing at once on the screen.

Another difference between the CAT and the traditional paper test is that you don't have to register months in advance. Instead, you take the CAT by appointment—which you can make even two days in advance—at an official test center. Simply call 800-GMAT-NOW (800-462-8669) in the United States and Canada or go to www.gmac.com or www.ets.org to register. You can also get the GMAT information application bulletin at a local college counseling office, library, or Kaplan Educational Center (800-KAP-TEST, that is, 800-527-8378; www.kaptest.com).

The CAT is offered six days a week, three weeks out of each month, at 400 testing centers. The centers are located at Sylvan Learning Centers, colleges and universities, and Educational Testing Service (ETS) offices. Hours and locations are available at www.gmac.com or www.ets.org, or by calling 800-GMAT-NOW (800-462-8669). There are some overseas centers as well. The test costs $190 in the United States, Puerto Rico, and U.S. territories, and slightly more in other countries.

Interpreting Your GMAT Score

GMAT score reports contain four separate scores: a quantitative score, a verbal score, an analytical writing score, and a total score. The quantitative and verbal subscores range from 0 to 60; in recent years, the average subscores have been between 28 and 39. Scores below 10 and above 46 are rare. Analytical writing scores go from 0 to 6 (6 being very high) in half-point increments. The recent average has been 3.9. The total score, which is what most people consider as their GMAT score, is based on the verbal and math scores and ranges from 200 to 800. The average total score hovers around 520.

Below, a few sample percentiles to help put these numbers (representing total scores) in context:

99th percentile—730 or above
95th—710
90th—680
80th—630
75th—610
50th—540

The score report lists your three most recent GMAT scores within the past five years. ETS, which creates and administers the test for the Graduate Management Admission Council, will report older scores if you request them but will add a cautionary note that those scores may not reflect your current abilities. If it's been five or more years, some schools may require you to retake the test.

As soon as you have finished the exam, you can choose to either see your unofficial score (which is almost always identical to the official one) or cancel it. If you cancel your test, it won't be scored and will appear on your GMAC report as a canceled score. No one, including you, will ever know how you did. Don't worry—B-schools won't think less of you for canceling a score. If you choose to see your score (which won't include your writing score—that will come with the official report), you can also select additional schools to which you would like your scores sent. The official score report should arrive at both the schools and your home within about two weeks of when you took the test.

> **INSIDER TIP.** You can pick five schools to send your scores to when you register for the GMAT. Even if you're not sure where you're applying, pick the most likely places; these first five score reports are free, but additional reports cost $25 each.

How Well Do You Have to Do?

Although exceptions are not unheard of, to be considered by a top-twenty school, you should aim to score at least a 600. But the scores at the very best programs are much higher: The average scores at Stanford and Wharton for the 2002 classes were 727 and 700, respectively. At *Business Week*'s thirtieth-ranked school, Georgia Tech, the average GMAT score was a respectable 635. However, schools also consider percentile scores in addition to numeric scores right now because the CAT is so new; the 90th to 99th percentile should earn you fair consideration at the top programs (see "Key Admissions Data" at the end of this chapter).

In general, the verbal and math subscores are less important than the total score, although some schools will look at the breakdown to see that a certain skill—usually quantitative—is up to snuff.

Many of the top schools will consider only your highest total score from a single test date. So if you got a 625 the first time you took the test and a 580 the second time, 625 will be the score they look at. Some schools will combine your highest verbal, quantitative, and total scores if they're from different test dates. A few will look at only your most recent scores, and others will average your scores. You're wise to ask schools about their policies before taking and retaking the test.

> **INSIDER TIP.** You may have heard the rumor that the top schools don't even look at the analytical writing sections of the test because they have such a huge load of applications to review. This is somewhat true—former admissions committee members of Harvard Business School and Wharton confirm that the writing score is generally only used to break a tie between two students. Moral of the story: Don't blow off the writing section. A stellar score can definitely help you if you're on the borderline.

Preparation Is Everything

Not to sound like your dear, sweet, nagging mother, but if you hope to do well on the GMAT, you really must prepare. By studying and familiarizing yourself with the test, you can definitely improve your score. For example, grammar questions constitute about 40 percent of the verbal section of the

GMAT. Haven't thought about dangling modifiers since eighth-grade English? Join the club. But you'll find that you can boost your score just by reviewing a few basic rules. Try to allot at least three months to study for the GMAT—although even a week or two is better than breezing into the test center unprepared.

The best method, as with any standardized test, is to practice with past exams. Consider purchasing *The Official Guide for GMAT Review (10th edition)*, published by GMAC/ETS. It's the only resource that contains official past GMATs. Or buy the PowerPrep software package, produced by ETS, which has two practice CATs made up of the same questions as in the *Official Guide*. (Shameless plug no. 214: You can also take a free GMAT diagnostic on mbajungle.com's "Getting In" channel.)

INSIDER TIP.   Few people know that ETS will actually allow you to take a practice GMAT CAT at one of the test centers. Definitely take advantage of this offer.

Unfortunately, the resources published by ETS contain only a few tests; you will probably need more practice tests than they provide. Also, these tests are from a few years ago and are somewhat dated. For example, some math concepts that were not on previous exams have been added in recent years.

That's a compelling argument for taking a GMAT course offered by a test-prep company like Kaplan or Princeton Review, both popular among business school applicants. Although test preparation has become an industry in itself—and these companies have a vested interest in getting you to believe that you need to take one of their classes in order to do well on the GMAT—it's their job to monitor the exam, identify common traps, and develop strategies for finding correct answers.

GMAT courses cost about $1,000, but they can be worth it if you go to all of the classes, work through most of the home-study material, take advantage of workshops, tutoring, and extra help sessions, and take simulated practice CATs at the test centers or on-line. (Keep in mind that these are tests created by the companies, so while they closely mimic the GMAT, your score on them and your experience with them won't quite be the same as an actual exam.)

The courses will generally brush you up on your skills, as well as help you understand the thinking behind the exam—something that can help you recognize types of problems faster, which of course may improve your score. Courses can also teach you how to approach the Analytical Writing Assessment, which is graded by both a person and a computer program called the "e-rater." Classes can teach you what the e-rater is looking for. At minimum, the courses will help you feel more comfortable come test day.

If you do decide to take a course, you will probably end up choosing between Kaplan and Princeton Review. They both offer books, study guides, diagnostic tests, homework books, on-line courses, and Kaplan has instructional materials on CD-ROM and video to supplement their classes. Kaplan also offers optional workshops on specific test topics and seminars about the application process.

Regardless of which company you choose—and especially if you elect not to use a company—there are a few additional things you can do to prepare for the test day:

Work on Your Endurance.   The GMAT is a long test, so you should take lots of practice tests. Being able to maintain concentration over several hours is key.

Simulate Test Conditions Exactly.   This includes practicing at the same time of day at which your test is scheduled, eating a meal at the same time you would on test day, and taking the scheduled breaks. Time yourself strictly, and don't cut out the writing section.

Review Your Practice Exams Thoroughly. Go over all of your answers—even the correct ones—and the explanations that your study guides provide. This will help reinforce concepts, formulas, and shortcuts.

Don't Work Just on Your Weaknesses. A point is a point, no matter where you get it, and you don't want your strengths to get rusty.

> **INSIDER TIP.** Take advantage of the simulated practice CATs and extra study sessions. In addition, a former Kaplan instructor advises: "Never be afraid to ask for anything, because people want to make you happy. They're very customer-service oriented."

Eight Tips for Test Day

1. Pick the Best Spot. If you live near multiple test centers, check them all out before registering, as some are quieter and more organized than others. Once you get there, make sure you have enough light, adequate space to write, and a comfortable chair. If you don't, ask for them. Also, make sure that your computer, mouse, and keyboard are working; you're given a short computer tutorial beforehand which should give you time to do this. The tutorial is also a good time to write down formulas, strategies, and mnemonic devices on your scratch paper.

2. Don't Cram the Day Before the Test. There's not much you can do to help yourself at this point, and you will just stress out. Review a few key points, gather what you will need for the next day, and take the night off.

3. Pack Reinforcements.   Besides the standard items like your admission ticket, a photo ID, and pencils or pens for scratch work, you'll want to bring a small snack and extra clothes with you. Dress in layers, as test centers are generally either too hot or too cold. Don't bring your own scratch paper, calculator, or digital watch—none of them are allowed. (Watches with hands are fine.) Your proctor will provide scratch paper, and there's a clock on your computer screen.

4. Pace Yourself.   Because the first five questions of each section are so important, start slowly (although there are limits to this if you are aiming for a very high score) and then speed up. The on-screen clock automatically stays on during the last five minutes of a section, but it can be turned on and off during the rest of the test. Turn it off during the first five questions so that you don't feel pressure while answering them.

5. Guess Strategically.   Guess only if you are truly stumped or tight on time. In either of these situations, you greatly improve your odds of answering the question correctly by eliminating at least one—and preferably two—wrong answers before guessing. If you have six to ten questions with less than five minutes left, try to eliminate at least one wrong answer before guessing. If you have eleven or more questions to go with less than five minutes left, guess randomly until you get to the last question, and spend all of your remaining time on that one.

6. Take a Break.   The CAT includes two optional five-minute breaks. Take them.

7. Don't Outsmart Yourself.   Don't get too caught up in your knowledge of how the test is scored and overanalyze the difficulty level of every question. If you get what seems like an easy question, don't panic: It might be a trick problem, an experimental question, or just one that's simple for you but hard for others. "Always concentrate on the question at hand," says one GMAT tutor. "Don't worry about the one before it or the one after it."

8. Don't Rush to Retake the Test. Of course, it's always possible that you will get flustered or have some other experience that causes you to score poorly on the test. But think twice before taking the GMAT again. Do you have a legitimate reason to think your score would improve a second time around? Did it diverge wildly from your scores on practice tests? Was your score low because you weren't familiar with the test format and types of questions? Do you have one or two clearly identifiable weaknesses that targeted study could improve? If so, you may be a good candidate to retake the test. The same holds true if there were extenuating circumstances—a personal trauma, illness, uncontrollable nerves, a poor night's sleep, or the guy next to you had a wet hacking cough and was bleeding from the eyebrows.

However, if you absolutely killed yourself studying the first time, you may be too burned out to do it all over again. Score jumps of 100 or more are unusual, and your score won't necessarily go up simply because you've taken the test before. If you've taken the GMAT twice or more already, you've probably done all the improving you're going to do.

THE MAN BEHIND THE GMAT:
INTERVIEW WITH A TEST-WRITER

Curious to know what kind of devious mind creates the seventy-eight questions that make up the GMAT? Meet John Hawthorn—gardener, cook, inquisitor extraordinaire. Now we get to ask the questions.

John Hawthorn earned a double major, in philosophy and physics, from Oxford and a Ph.D. from McGill University.

by S. Kirk Walsh

But when his wife's work moved them from Hawaii to Pennsylvania, even this collection of degrees couldn't land him the type of teaching job he was after. So the forty-nine-year-old Brit thought about his assets—a deep reservoir of knowledge, intellectual curiosity, a proclivity toward quizzing young minds—and soon found himself at the Educational Testing Service in Princeton, New Jersey, where for nine years he's been one of thirty-five GMAT question writers. Here, Hawthorn fields a few of our questions:

Trace the path of a question from start to finish.

We have twenty or so outside writers around the world who submit material from a broad field of topics they find in reasonably intelligent publications, such as *The Economist* and *History Today*. For example, we may use reporting from the *Wall Street Journal* about a company's attempts to increase its market share by lowering prices. We try to turn that company's decisionmaking process into a topic for a question, which someone in-house writes up. The question is then examined internally and by outside reviewers—usually business school professors. If it passes this process, it's included in a real test, but it's not scored.

Do most questions pass?

About 40 percent fail to make it into the official test.

How many questions do you write in a day?

Three or four, but I can also sweat and sweat and barely write one.

What's the best question you've ever written?

It's not my best question, but it's the one I love the most. It was about Simpson's paradox—about how the average of averages can be a misleading statistic. I came up with a killer way to construct it, which was something like this: Suppose that oranges are grown in two areas—one that's very fertile and another that isn't. And suppose that over a ten-year period the productivity of each area, measured in crates of oranges per acre of grove, increases. You might think that overall productivity of oranges must also increase. In fact, it doesn't have to. If the acreage of orange groves in the not-so-fertile area has also increased, overall productivity can actually decrease. The question made it into the test, but it sank. No one understood it.

What's the hardest type of question to write?

The easiest questions are the hardest to write because they have to be very clear. We all have a tendency to make something a little too clever. So I say to myself, "I will make this question as easy as I can." Naturally this goes against the grain. For example, if I'm focusing on a company with a specific goal, there may be several details involved in its strategy, and I really have to focus on one straightforward element to make the question easy. And that's not so easy.

Do you think of the test takers when you write questions?

Yes, very much. In particular, we want to make sure that we aren't unfair to any group of test takers by relying on specific knowledge or attitude.

What is the training for becoming a question writer?

Writers tend to have academic background, but it's not required. There is an in-house training session that covers the technical aspects of statistics, our practices for writing questions, and our editorial policies. There is also training in fairness standards so that writers don't come up with questions that are gender or race biased. It usually takes about six months for a new writer to get up to speed.

Is there competition among the writers?

No, it's an amazingly cooperative group. You do take a certain amount of pride in the work you've done, but usually someone rewrites a question. In the end, your name may be on it, but you don't recognize the question. It can be quite humbling.

What's the salary of an entry-level writer?

If someone has a Ph.D., usually around $48,000.

Do you think of questions while you're in the shower?

I think about them all the time.

Do you think about how people struggle with your questions while they're taking the test?

Yes, I feel great sympathy for people who have to take the test in a real-time situation. I honestly admire people who do it well.

Really? Then think fast. If the width of a rectangle is increased by 10 percent and the length is decreased by 20 percent, by what percent does the area decrease?
  A. 2 percent
  B. 12 percent
  C. 16 percent
  D. 20 percent
  E. 21 percent

Ohhhhh. Wow. Nasty. What are my choices again?

A. 2 percent, B. 12 percent, C. 16 percent, D. 20 percent, E. 21 percent.

I'll pick 12 percent, but I'm not a mathematician.

You got it.

WHAT DOES IT TAKE TO GET IN?

Key Admissions Data

Ranking	Business School	Avg. GMAT	GMAT range	Under-grad Avg. GPA	Appli-cations Accepted
1	U. Pennsylvania (Wharton)	700	640-750	3.5	14%
2	Northwestern (Kellogg)	690	NA	3.45	18%
3	Harvard	701	NA	3.5	13%
4	MIT (Sloan)	703	650-760	3.5	17%
5	Duke (Fuqua)	690	640-720	3.33	19%
6	U. of Michigan	677	620-730	3.34	21%
7	Columbia	704	640-750	3.45	12%
8	Cornell (Johnson)	673	620-730	3.43	25%
9	U. Virginia (Darden)	676	600-730	3.26	19%
10	U. of Chicago	684	630-740	3.43	25%
11	Stanford	727	690-770	3.56	8%
12	UCLA (Anderson)	698	640-710	3.6	15%
13	NYU (Stern)	686	640-740	3.4	22%
14	Carnegia Mellon	660	600-730	3.2	31%
15	UNC-Chapel Hill (Flagler)	667	600-740	3.27	22%
16	Dartmouth (Tuck)	692	640-740	3.4	14%
17	UT-Austin (McCombs)	687	570-790	3.4	25%
18	UC-Berkeley (Haas)	684	620-750	3.54	14%
19	Yale	687	640-740	3.48	17%
20	U. of Indiana (Kelley)	646	580-710	3.32	32%
21	U. Rochester (Simon)	646	600-690	3.2	30%
22	Vanderbilt (Owen)	690	580-720	3.2	38%
23	Washington U. (Olin)	701	610-730	3.18	29%
24	USC (Marshall)	703	610-720	3.3	27%
25	Purdue (Krannert)	690	550-730	3.22	23%
26	Georgetown (McDonough)	677	635-670	3.23	19%
27	U. Maryland (Smith)	704	600-700	3.3	23%
28	Emory (Goizueta)	673	600-730	3.4	34%
29	Michigan State (Broad)	676	580-720	3.35	26%
30	Georgia Tech (DuPree)	684	590-670	3.2	35%

Source: Business Week, U.S. News, Financial Times   (of those attending)   (middle 80% of those accepted)   (of those attending)   (of total applications)

Other Top 50 Schools

Business School	Avg. GMAT	GMAT range	Under-grad Avg. GPA	Appli-cations Accepted
U. Minnesota (Carlson)	640	560-710	3.3	33%
Ohio State (Fisher)	645	598-700	3.26	29%
U. Arizona (Eller)	644	600-710	3.5	12%
Arizona State	635	570-710	3.3	35%
Tulane (Freeman)	644	570-740	3.4	39%
Case Western (Weatherhead)	618	520-710	3.19	51%
Penn State (Smeal)	608	N/A	3.27	N/A
Rice (Jones)	640	550-710	3.11	39%
Thunderbird	608	550-690	3.39	76%
U. Wisconsin-Madison	620	560-720	3.3	26%
Boston College (Carroll)	645	550-710	3.3	40%
U. California-Irvine	664	620-720	3.37	33%
BYU (Marriott)	642	560-710	3.53	38%
Southern Methodist	644	590-700	3.2	33%
Texas A&M (Mays)	628	560-690	3.33	24%
U. California-Davis	673	610-740	3.2	31%
Wake Forest (Babcock)	645	580-710	3.2	51%
U. Georgia (Terry)	645	580-710	3.18	28%
U. Illinois-Champaign	621	560-712	3.3	43%
Notre Dame (Mendoza)	639	580-730	3.2	29%

Source: Business Week, U.S. News, Financial Times

(of those attending)   (middle 80% of those accepted)   (of those attending)   (of total applications)

Business School	Country	Avg. GMAT	GMAT range	Applications Accepted
INSEAD	France	688	N/A	N/A
London Business School	England	690	630-700	32%
IESE	Spain	655	590-720	31%
IMD	Switzerland	650	530-750	13%
University of Western Ontario (Ivey)	Canada	661	590-740	40%
Rotterdam School	Netherlands	622	550-690	40%
Toronto (Rotman)	Canada	674	620-740	31%
SDA Bocconi	Italy	640	560-780	22%
Melbourne School	Australia	640	550-730	35%
Chinese University of Hong Kong	China	600	540-710	30%
International University of Japan	Japan	550	400-680	75%
McGill University	Canada	639	590-650	35%
DUXX	Mexico	550	450-680	6%
Theseus	France	620	550-720	24%
University of Manchester	England	610	540-690	52%
Waseda University		550	480-750	65%
ESADE	Spain	660	590-760	16%
Queens University	Canada	674	620-730	27%

Source: Financial Times, Business Week

5

Are You Ready for B-School?
Are You Sure?

....

CALM BEFORE THE STORM

You receive a fat envelope. The love is flowing both ways. You accept the offer and send in your deposit. Now what?

Some people spend the summer before school traveling hither and yon. If you can swing it, it's obviously an attractive option. After all, it may be one of the last chances to chuck your obligations—and your long pants—and take some serious time off. At the same time, lots of people work pretty much until the week they start school, earning money or completing projects before going back into student mode. As one Columbia '99 MBA recalls: "I came back to New York from a business trip, basically got off the plane and went to class."

Whether you have the luxury to go on a long vacation is for you to decide, but there are clear benefits to taking at least a few weeks off before beginning school. If you are like most incoming students, you haven't attended a lecture or sharpened a pencil in five years, and a return to a life divided into class periods can be a culture shock. Not to mention the distress you may feel as you are asked to perform derivatives or other statistical analyses that you haven't done in years, if *ever*.

MBA Boot Camp

It goes without saying that you should take some time to spank up your skills. If you studied economics, math, or accounting, dig up ye olde textbooks and reread—or reskim—them. For many, however, the do-it-yourself model isn't really a viable option.

What then? You can almost always find a summer course or minicourse at a local school or college. However, the best place to look is often your business school. Many now offer or require some sort of pre-term preparation in business basics. Wharton, for example, offers a month-long pre-term of courses ranging from statistics to accounting to history. The Thunderbird School in Arizona offers a week of brushup before the formal schooling begins. Notre Dame and many other business schools also give basic quant training.

Though they are only the appetizers, pre-terms are there for a reason: to prepare students quickly and efficiently for the busy pace of graduate-school life. One student compares the first semester to "learning five languages at once," so the more you can do to help yourself before the first day of class, the better. In fact, pre-term may not just be an option: many B-schools *require* you to take economics, calculus, and statistics before you arrive. But even if your school doesn't demand it, familiarity with these subjects can give you a head start. If you're not quite ready for calculus, college-level algebra is the bare minimum.

And then there's the whole computer thing. Knowing how to use Microsoft Word is a given. Microsoft Excel is the de facto standard for financial modeling, and PowerPoint is essential for developing dynamic electronic presentations. Most schools offer tutorials in these, but any extra skills you have will definitely go a long way. Finally, e-mail and Internet skills are absolutely necessary. Most school-to-student communication now goes through e-mail, and you'll have to navigate syllabi and company research on-line. Without these basic Internet skills, you will struggle from Day One.

> INSIDER TIP. Even if you have strong quantitative skills, you may want to consider taking refresher courses. Why? It could help you place out of core classes—which could work to your advantage down the line (see "Choosing the Curriculum: Electives Versus the Core," Chapter 6).

Summer Plans: The Have-Your-Cake Option

Before you decide whether you will take the entire summer off or work until the first day of class, consider a couple of options that have become popular over the last few years. The first is some sort of part-time solution. One Michigan MBA, for example, got her boss to agree to engage her on a consulting basis: roughly twenty hours per week, on her own schedule. This allowed her to study up as well as take time to visit family and friends across the country. Part-time is a great way to keep making money, to catch up on skills, and to transition smoothly to the next phase of life.

Another option increasingly being pursued is the internship. In this case, you quit your job in early summer to do a two-month stint at a different company (usually in a different industry), ending just before school. This is an especially attractive option for students who are accepted into school early, since they have a lot of time to find a great summer opportunity. It's not always easy, but landing a summer job can have serious benefits: You get to try a new industry or company virtually risk free. You can beef up your resumé—a big advantage when recruiting season rolls around. The people you meet will only add to your network of contacts. Of course, there's always the chance that you'll find yourself a great situation, and a great job after graduation.

Finally, many use the summer to pursue volunteer work, which is good for the soul and good for the resumé. This is a variation on the part-time option, since it generally allows a fair amount of time for studying and relaxing.

EIGHT BOOKS YOU GOTTA READ BEFORE B-SCHOOL

1. *Liar's Poker,* **by Michael Lewis**. An astute, well-written portrayal of the world of Wall Street traders, circa the roaring '80s. Full of juicy tidbits, ripe jargon, and solid insights into Street life. Also, I-banker types will be quoting various scenes from the book, so you might as well be able play along. Best of all, it's just a great read.

2. *The Art of War,* **by Sun Tzu.** Is there a CEO who *hasn't* read this? The basic tenets of strategy—how you defeat your opponent—remain constant over time, and this is a classic interpretation.

3. *The Goal,* **by Eliyahu M. Goldratt.** A bit earnest, yes, but a superb introduction to the almost sexy world of operations. In novel form, readers are walked though a manufacturing facility where anything that ever could go wrong has gone wrong. At every turn, we get new ideas on the right way to run a business. Warning: After reading *The Goal,* you may start inserting the word "throughput" into your everyday conversations.

4. **A basic accounting primer or textbook.** Sorry, it ain't all fun, games, and fast-moving sentences. If you give yourself a few hours to get (re)acquainted with accounting, you'll be way ahead of the game come September.

5. *A Random Walk Down Wall Street,* **by Burton G. Malkiel.** A classic—at least in the eyes of just about

every finance professor on the planet. An eye-opening and controversial look at theories and facts behind the world of investing.

6. *Getting to Yes*, by **Roger Fisher and William Ury.** One of the best-known and widely read works on the art of negotiation. A quick read, but the ideas will keep you thinking long afterward. Because what is business if not negotiation?

7. *Built to Last*, by **James C. Collins and Jerry I. Porras.** The authors make their case as to why certain companies (such as Disney, Motorola, Merck) have outperformed their peers over the years. It's a book that tends to elicit strong opinions. Some hail it as revelatory and inspiring. Others call it a fluffed-up retread of *In Search of Excellence*, by Thomas Peters. Whatever your verdict, it's a book that professors tend to assign in management, leadership, and entrepreneurship classes.

8. *Harry Potter and the Mixed-Up Wizard of Leveraged Buyouts*. Our young hero gets in over his head and wrestles with Golden Parachutes and Poison Pills. Large-type version available.

READY TO TALK THE TALK?

One Hundred Terms to Know Before You Get to B-School

1. **Add value** To improve the bottom line
2. **Air hog** A loudmouth student who constantly competes for airtime in class
3. **Airtime** What air hogs battle for—gained by making comments in class largely to get the professor's attention

4. **Analysis paralysis** The condition of having so much information that it becomes difficult to make a decision

5. **B2B, B2C, C2C, P2P** Acronyms for different Internet business models: business-to-business (VerticalNet), business-to-consumer (Amazon.com), consumer-to-consumer (eBay), peer-to-peer (Napster) (Note: After the dot-com implosion, B2B has taken on a new meaning: back-to-banking. B2C? Back-to-consulting.)

6. **Back-bencher** Someone who sits in the back row of a class making fun of other students

7. **Back-of-the-envelope** Quick and dirty analysis, also "BOE"

8. **Bandwidth** The capacity to take in new information

9. **Barriers to entry** Characteristics of a company or industry that make it difficult for new competitors to succeed

10. **Beer blast** Come on. You remember. Like in college?

11. **Beta** Measure of a stock's volatility

12. **Block** The group of students with whom you take most of your first-year classes. Also: "section" and "cohort"

13. **Brand** Sum of how consumers perceive a company, its products and services, and its image

14. **Burn rate** The rate at which a company expends capital before it generates positive cash flow

15. **Chip shots** Comments made in class solely for the purpose of gaining airtime

16. **Click-through rate** The percentage of people who see an ad on a web site who then click on that ad; a measure of success

17. **Cold call** Method of teaching in many business school courses where a professor randomly selects a student to discuss a business case you were sup-

posed to know about (i.e., "Professor Xavier cold calls, so you better read the case before class.")

18. **Cost-benefit analysis** A technique used to quantify the tangible and intangible upsides and downsides of a project

19. **Cycle time** The period of time required to turn something around

20. **Deliverable** Final product

21. **Ding,** or **ding letter** Rejection call or letter after a job interview

22. **Drill down** To take a specific issue within a larger one and subject it to a more thorough analysis or assessment

23. **Drivers** The key variables of analysis that have the greatest impact

24. **80-20** A method of prioritizing (i.e., "Eighty percent of the sales comes from 20 percent of the clients, so let's focus on them.")

25. **Exit strategy** A way out of a business situation, good or bad—often refers to an IPO or acquisition by another company

26. **Finhead** Finance head. See also: number cruncher, gearhead, quant jock

27. **The five forces** Michael Porter's model for analyzing the strategic attractiveness of an industry

28. **Four Ps** Elements of a marketing strategy: price, promotion, place, product

29. **Fume date** Date a company will run out of cash reserves

30. **Fundamentals** The basic information on a company or stock, such as revenues, price-to-earnings ratio, earnings per share, and so on

31. **Gearhead** Someone with a technical background . . . and not much else

32. **Globalization** The process of expanding a market or a business to adapt to multicountry, multiconsumer economics

33. **Glocal** Business strategy of being both global and local at the same time
34. **Going forward** In the future
35. **Guerrilla marketing** An unconventional promotional strategy
36. **Gunner** Someone who is constantly raising his hand in class
37. **Hard courses** Quantitatively based classes
38. **Holding cost** Cost of owning unsold inventory
39. **HP-19-B** B-school calculator of choice
40. **I-bankers** Students who have either just come from an analyst program at an investment bank or who plan to enter investment banking after graduation
41. **Incentivize** Motivate
42. **Inflection point** A dramatic change in a key variable such as a company's valuation due to a particular cause or event
43. **IPO** Initial public offering
44. **Leverage** To use to your advantage
45. **Linear programming** Analysis performed to determine optimal combination of multiple inputs or variables
46. **Liquidity event** An event (generally an IPO, a buyout, or a merger) that allows investors to convert their holdings into cash
47. **Low-hanging fruit** Obvious opportunities that are easy to leverage
48. **Making traction** Making modest progress
49. **Marketing myopia** Strategic error in judgment regarding the nature of an industry or a market
50. **McJob** A low-paying position, often in the service industry
51. **Mindshare** Percentage of available attention dedicated to an idea
52. **Mock** Simulated interview, usually with second-years interviewing first-years (also used as a verb)

53. **Monetize** To drive revenue from an idea, product, technology, or service. Shorthand for "make money from it."

54. **Mosh pit** Library study area prior to final exams

55. **Net income** Profits

56. **Net net** Income after deducting all expenses, including insurance and maintenance costs

57. **Net present value (NPV)** Used both in its literal sense (i.e., the current value of future earnings) and colloquially to describe something or someone that will make a lot of money (i.e. "That's a high-NPV idea"; "She has a high NPV.")

58. **Number cruncher** Someone who excels at quantitative analysis; tends to refer to a person who is more an executor than a strategic thinker

59. **Off-line** Outside of a class or meeting (i.e. "Let's not take up everyone's time with that issue; we can discuss it off-line.")

60. **One-off** On a one-time or case-by-case basis

61. **On-line** During a class or meeting

62. **Opportunity costs** The cost of not pursuing a given project

63. **OOC** Out of cash

64. **Outliers** Pieces of information so different from the rest of the data that you disregard them

65. **P/E** Abbreviation for the price-to-earnings ratio of a stock; a way to gauge a stock's value

66. **Poet** A student with little or no analytical background

67. **Plug and chug** To run spreadsheets; what I-bankers spend their time doing

68. **Pre-enrollment courses** (also **pre-terms**) Classes offered the summer before the first year of business school

69. **Pro forma** The presentation of hypothetical financial information based on certain assumptions; often used in business plans

70. **PTI** Pre-tax income
71. **Pushback** to disagree, offer resistance or a counterargument
72. **Quant jock** Someone with an analytical background whose strength is crunching numbers
73. **Regression analysis** Statistical analysis performed to determine correlation among specific variables
74. **Risk-reward trade-off** The idea that there is a proportional relationship between the level of risk and the potential for reward
75. **ROI** Shorthand for "return on investment." How much you profit (or lose) in percentage terms on a given investment
76. **Run the numbers** To perform a thorough quantitative analysis
77. **Scalable** Used to describe an application or a business model that can adapt to an infinite number of customers
78. **Share of voice** The portion of total media within a category that a brand generates; also **share of market** (percentage of total category sales a brand generates) and **share of wallet** (amount of a consumer's budget allocated to a product)
79. **Sharks** Aggressive students in a class discussion or during interactions with corporate recruiters
80. **Six sigma** A popular corporate process for identifying and measuring defects in a product in order to eliminate them
81. **Soft courses** Nonanalytical courses such as personnel management and organizational change
82. **Soft skills** Nonanalytical skills such as conflict resolution, leadership, and communication
83. **Stickiness** The ability of a web site to keep visitors from leaving the site
84. **Strategic imperative** A requirement for success

85. **Sunk cost** Money or effort wasted in the past that should be ignored when assessing the current situation

86. **SWOT** Strength, weakness, opportunity, threat. A framework for conducting case analysis

87. **Synergy** The effective combination of two or more actions or projects that is greater than the sum of its parts.

88. **Take-away** Key point(s) of a meeting or analysis

89. **10,000 feet** Very broad analysis of a business situation

90. **The three Cs** A method by which to approach a problem; refers to customer, competition, company (there is also the four Cs method: customer, competition, cost, capacity)

91. **Time-value of money** The notion that money today is worth more than money tomorrow

92. **To have legs** To have long-term potential; to be worthy of further consideration. Usually used in regard to an idea

93. **Top-line** Initial analysis of an issue or information

94. **Top quartile** Top 25 percent of performance or outcomes

95. **Total quality management** Derived from the Edward Demming method of management; a process of continuous improvement in order to boost customer satisfaction

96. **Upside** Potential benefits of a business transaction; opposite: downside

97. **Valuation** A way to assess the current value of a business; may be accomplished by analyzing projected future cash flows or looking at the value of comparable companies

98. **Value-added** An enhancement to a product or service that increases its value to the consumer

99. **Value proposition** Core service or value that compels the customer or client to respond to your product or service
100. **Viral** A method by which ideas are spread from one user to another like a virus

WHAT TO BRING TO THE PARTY— THE TOOLS, THE GEAR, THE ATTITUDE

Your most precious commodities come with you, of course: your brain, your skills, your experience, your dashing good looks. For everything else you need to hit the ground running, you have this list:

Backpack. Business school doesn't only test your mental strength, it tests your ability to haul cereal-box-size books and multiple three-ring binders around a mile-wide campus. Invest in a strong backpack that will hold a laptop computer, books, calculator, and an electronic organizer—all without crushing your international marketing report. Forget fashion: Leather bags are too heavy, and over-the-shoulder bags and briefcases are difficult to manage when you're sprinting to class or riding a bike. You will want a briefcase or nice shoulder bag for interview season; a backpack slung over a $600 suit just doesn't cut it. Or pick up an attractive leather portfolio. When you interview, you can drop your backpack at the door and carry your resumé and other important papers in style.

Basic Supplies. Anyone who's used to raiding the company supply closet on a regular basis is in for a rude awakening on the first visit to Office Depot. Binders, notebooks, papers, Post-it notes are not cheap. A few weeks after school starts,

by Deirdre O'Scannlain

you'll be hooked into the pen-pipeline care of visiting recruiters, but you *will* have to buy binders, notebooks, and
portfolios. The most cost-effective strategy is to buy a few
odds and ends to get you through the first couple of days, then
decide what you really need for each class before you splurge.
Do invest in a nice pen for taking notes during interviews—
you don't want to whip out a cheap ballpoint inscribed with a
competitor's name when a job is on the line. As for tape
recorders, leave them at home. Most classes grade on participation, so you're better off present than at home deciphering
a tape. If you have to miss a class, many are videotaped and
available at the library. Or there's always getting the notes
from a friendly classmate.

Digital Organizer.   While you can certainly get by without one, especially if you're used to a trusty Week-at-a-
Glance, you'll appreciate any help you can get keeping
classes, recruiting events, team meetings, and interviews
straight. Another bonus: You can use it to inconspicuously
read the news or play games when a class gets boring. A PDA
is also great for quickly storing contact names. Your classmates are your best assets the first semester—the more
names and numbers you input, the greater the chance you'll
get help on an accounting question at 11 P.M. the night before it's due. Be sure to type in all of your past and current
business and personal contacts as well. The top PDA picks
now? A Handspring Visor (the Prism with color display is
tasty) or Palm VII, both with beaming capability. By the way,
beaming is huge. Huge!

Laptop Computer.   Before you go charging out to buy the
latest and greatest PC laptop, contact your school. Some universities—Michigan, to name just one—have such well-
stocked computer facilities that you may be able to get by
without one your first year. At most programs, having your
own computer is key, but call anyway for guidance on laptop

specs. Sloan (MIT), for instance, simply requires that you get a Windows-compatible laptop with at least 128 megs of RAM, 500 megahertz Pentium processor, and ten gigabytes of hard disk. Other schools, such as Northwestern Kellogg, are more specific and have a certain brand they offer to students at a discount.

Financial Calculator.   Yes, you will be analyzing net present value, derivatives, and interest rates. Fortunately, you will have a calculator, like a Hewlett-Packard HP-19bii, to help you. These souped-up machines are not cheap, however, so wait until you know exactly which one you'll need before you buy it. This information will either be mailed to you before classes begin or explained the first day of class.

Interview Suits.   Let's not kid ourselves. The number-one goal at B-school is landing a great job when you graduate, right? So don't go spending $60,000-plus on school and skimp on your interview attire. An adequate suit will cost at least $600, a good suit, up to twice—or three times—as much. While it seems like a fortune to spend on clothing, remember that you will most likely wear suits for your summer internship, a job after graduation, interviews the next five years, and entertaining clients. In all of these situations, it never hurts to look good.

While you can probably get by with one, it's best to have two suits so you can wear something different to the round-two interview. Expensive models are generally worth the money. They travel well, require less pressing, last longer, and, perhaps most important, give you a more polished appearance. Buy conservative: Choose dark blue or gray, and avoid eye-catching stripes or, heaven forbid, fabrics with a glossy sheen. Men should bring at least three silk ties. Better-quality shoes and belts, like a suit, last a long time and are worth the money. In addition to their suits or conservative

---

SIX THINGS YOU CAN LEAVE AT HOME

- Poster that says "If you're not wasted, the day is!"
- Ray Liotta Doll
- That small bag of hair
- "Saved by the Bell" lunch box
- Imaginary Friend "Smitty"
- Propensity to sing "Party All the Time" in public

---

skirts, women should also remember to pack a dress for dances and other semiformal occasions. A word of caution: Some companies conduct casual interviews, so make sure you have a few pairs of nice slacks and a sport coat.

An Iron, Lint Brush, and Shoe-Shine Kit.   This would seem fairly self-explanatory, no?

Personal Cards.   What's more compelling: Handing a contact a printed personal card or scribbling your name on a scrap of notebook paper? You guessed it. Cards won't have much of an impact in interviews, but they're very handy for conferences, presentations, and other networking events. Check with the student affairs office to see if your school has a standard. If not, keep them simple and conservative. Your name, phone number, and e-mail address are just fine. Remember to use a cell phone number (if you don't already have a cell phone, check with the school about a reduced-rate plan) and e-mail address. Good cards will set you back around $80—you might as well throw in another $150 or so for personal stationery to have on hand for thank-you letters.

An E-mail Address.   In addition to whatever e-mail you already have, get yourself a Hotmail or Yahoo! account so people will be able to contact you easily when you move.

Sports Equipment.   Play tennis, golf, run, or ski? Bring all of your gear unless you know that you will absolutely, positively not use it. You'll find an intramural club or team for just about every sport imaginable, and time spent playing is a necessary stress buster.

Bike.   A bike will come in handy at just about every school. But remember, college campuses are ground zero for bike theft. Unless you plan on doing any serious mountain biking on weekends, pick up something cheap and functional—and save your money for a strong, lightweight lock.

Passport.   Get one, or make sure your current passport hasn't expired. Business school offers many opportunities for world travel, including class trips, internships abroad, and vacation with your friends. You won't want to stand in line at the post office—or deal with State Department bureaucracy, for that matter—in order to leave for spring break.

Computer Skills.   Remember scoffing at your company's nerdy all-day tutorials on Microsoft Word, Excel, and Power-Point? Well, it's time to change your tune and sign up: You simply cannot get through your first year without solid word-processing, spreadsheet, and, to a lesser extent, presentation skills—and if you can take these classes for free, all the better. If your company does not offer tutorials or you've already resigned, buy a book and polish up these skills at home.

A Good Read.   By staying current with financial and world news, you'll not only be better prepared for your class work but will be armed against recruiters who are eager to test your knowledge. A favorite interview question: "I've been on vacation for the last week, and I need you to fill me in on what's going on in the financial markets and international affairs. Go." Subscribe to the *Wall Street Journal* and the *New York Times* no matter what career you're pursuing. If concentrating in finance, you'll also want to peruse *Barron's* and the *Financial Times*. For e-business, check out the *Industry Standard*. Zeroing in on a particular industry? Sign up for the top trade publication in that field. (And statistics prove that reading *MBA Jungle* will increase your salary by $37,024.03 every six months.)

A Plan.   You're in the trenches now: Take advantage of it. Have you conceived of a business plan or been hit with the entrepreneurial muse? Jot down notes and take them with you to school. No matter how rough, half-baked, or downright silly, these bits of inspiration will be pure gold when you're overworked and in desperate need of a paper topic. Print out any reports—or even e-mails—you're proud of so you can remember important points that might pertain to class projects.

6

B2C—Back to the Classroom

···

WHATEVER YOUR EXPECTATIONS ARE OF BUSINESS SCHOOL, YOU CAN BE PRETTY SURE THAT THE EXPERIENCE WILL BE DIFFERENT THAN YOU THOUGHT. FOR ONE THING, THERE ARE SEEMING CONTRADICTIONS AT every turn. Your professors may be brilliant, but you will often learn more from your fellow classmates. You are competing against others but at the same time working closely with them. Your classmates come to school with different professional backgrounds but are expected to learn and grow as one. You buy $700 suits to look good for interviews but eat at the falafel stand down the street to save a few bucks. You just took a major break from your career, but one of the first things you really focus on is finding a job. You will navigate all of these contradictions and others in due course, and you will come out the better for it, with the tools, savvy insights, and networks to achieve all of your professional goals.

START SMART, START STRONG: WHAT TO GET DONE IN YOUR FIRST TWO MONTHS AT SCHOOL

Consider, just for a moment, an Olympic long-distance track event. Each runner is in top physical condition and has been training for the race for years. And even though the race consists of more than six miles—just over twenty-five times around the track—the first few hundred yards are considered among the most important. Because it is during those first moments that each runner establishes her position. Can you establish a good position late in the race? Of course. But it is considerably more difficult to do so, and the savvy competitor understands how crucial it is to start strong. And so it is with B-school. The first two months are critical to the two years that follow. Below, a checklist to keep you on your stride.

Before Your First Day
- Housing basics: phone, cable, utility services, and so forth.
- Local bank/checking account. See if the school has a deal with one that offers free ATM or free checking.
- Locate nearby Laundromat and dry cleaner.
- Find a local Kinko's or other place to do copying. Make friends with the manager. Buy him coffee or lunch or a bottle of expensive wine. You want this guy to like you.
- Join school or other gym; identify a place to run/play squash/tennis/golf/whatever. Definitely get a locker so you don't have to drag your gym stuff around with you on top of your books and laptop.
- Wander around the neighborhood, take stock of local stores (locksmith, passport photos, stationery store, post office, etc.). Spending an hour now will save you countless hours later.
- Pick up as many restaurant delivery menus as you can.
- Set up your laptop with Word, Excel, and Power-Point; configure modem if necessary.

The First Week
- Get scholarship, tuition, and loan paperwork processed.
- Score any parking permits you need and maybe a few you don't.
- Familiarize yourself with school health-care facilities and services.

- Figure out if you can take any placement exams that would allow you to place out of core courses.
- Establish daily calendar.
- Learn where classrooms and buildings are.
- Find out how to reserve rooms for team meeting.
- Pick up a copy of the school directory with office and emergency phone numbers.
- Get school-based e-mail address; learn everything you can about the school e-mail system.
- Buy a calculator: the HP-19-B is considered the best. Students (and bankers) love it because it allows you to pre-program formulas.
- Arrange your Palm or other PDA. Whatever system you use, *get your calendar organized now*. Seriously, don't put this off. We don't want to have to ask you again.

Weeks Two Through Four
- Get school-based Internet connection and home dial-up.
- Buy business cards. They are often available through the school; if not, get your own.
- Go to presentation or organization meetings for four to six clubs (marketing, entrepreneurs, women in business, etc.).
- Find a killer coffee place.
- Read ahead in class—falling behind, especially in subjects like accounting and statistics is a major stress-builder. You will have enough stress as it is.
- Sign up for any interesting seminars or events.
- Go to a company presentation just to familiarize yourself with the routine.
- Identify a quiet place to sit and read or study.
- Find a couple of classmates with similar interests. No, not career stuff. You know, like movies, hockey, golf, music, knitting, yoga, rebuilding airplane engines using only dental floss and a pitchfork.

- Have an informal get-to-know-you event with your learning team (like watching old episodes of *Survivor*); agree on rules and objectives.
- Establish a basic work plan for yourself: when you are going to get work done, research your job, work out, sleep, eat. Doing this is important; it will help you rise to the challenge of the demands of the first semester and not be overwhelmed by them.

Over the Next Month
- Get to know the key people in the career resource center, and consider kissing up.
- Learn how the career center works and what the rules are.
- Begin to focus on your target industry or industries. Get a list of companies that come to campus and identify the ones you want to investigate.
- Find out which second-year students worked at companies you're interested in.
- Review your resumé; take a first cut at the new version and get feedback from second-year students and/or the school career development staff.
- Buy lots of resumé paper, envelopes, and stamps.
- Start researching your potential area of career direction: Get industry guides from school and clubs. You can also access free industry guides and company profiles at—hold on to your hats, folks—mbajungle.com.
- Join two to three clubs and get involved with one of them; specifically, become a first-year officer, help to organize an event.
- Get to know a couple of your professors outside of class. Some schools subsidize lunch or coffee with profs—take advantage of it and schedule early.
- Go to a few events where you can meet and interact with second-years: build relationships with them so you can seek their advice later. You will need it.

CLASS IN THE CLASSROOM

For most people, the return to the classroom will be a distinct culture shock. After all, it's been quite a few years since you were last in this kind of environment. At this point, you know how to manage employees, how to manage the management, and generally what it takes to be successful in the workplace. The classroom, however, is an entirely different beast.

General Etiquette

Unless you are detained due to work or interviewing, it's best not to come late to class. Professors' attitudes toward tardiness range from annoyance to much less forgiving, and it can be disruptive to your fellow students as well. Most schools have rules against food in the classroom, which are pretty much universally disregarded. From an etiquette point of view, coffee and donuts are usually fine, but don't bring your Happy Meal into the classroom—unless you want to have your proverbial lunch handed to you. If you have to leave class early for an interview, it's a good idea to e-mail the professor or just tell him before class starts.

Speak Up, Sonny

As a business school student, you are definitely expected to contribute—in most classes, your participation will be rated, and there is no way to get top grades without strong marks in this area. Be advised that quantity is not necessarily quality here. Remember that you are surrounded by smart people—who notice right away if you're just filling the air with articulate versions of "me too." Make sure you have something substantive to contribute and a rationale that supports your point of view. It is fair game for a professor (or fellow student) to probe for this, and to publicly question your logic. But even if you're filled with razor-sharp insights, don't hog the airspace—it's considered very bad etiquette and people will call you nasty names behind your back and stick pins in a little doll that has your name on it. Especially in classes where a large portion of the grade is dependent on participation, dominating the time will not particularly endear you to other students, and professors also like to spread it around a bit. A good guideline is to try and make one or two substantive comments in each class every week.

If you don't understand something a professor is saying, chances are others are confused too. So feel free to ask for clarification. This certainly does not count against you. Of course, if you're not understanding something because you were thinking about your withering stock portfolio, you may want to come back to it later with a friend.

A VERY SPECIAL WARNING.   A small but nontrivial contingent of professors "cold call" in class. This means that even though you did not raise your hand, sat in the back of the class, and wore camouflage clothing, the professor can call your name and ask you, in front of the entire class, what you think about a given problem.

Two tricks for you to keep in mind. First—duh—prepare. It will be painfully obvious if you do not. Assuring that you're ready to discuss the issue at hand is really why most professors cold call in the first place. Second, keep in mind that the professor is not trying to make you look stupid; rather he or she simply wants to keep the discussion moving at a good clip. If you say something that turns out to be wrong, that's just part of the process of moving toward the right answer.

THE CASE STUDY

A Favorite Teaching Method.   If you have never heard of a "case study," you will shortly, and you'll see enough of them to last you quite a while. Basically, a case is intended to be a rough proxy of a real business situation, and a given case can illustrate issues pertaining to just about any aspect of business, from marketing to finance, from corporate strategy to business psychology. Harvard pioneered the use of cases, figuring that if they drilled you enough with these simulations, you'd be better prepared when you faced the real thing. Now almost all business schools use the case method to some extent—most of them written by Harvard professors. (Along the way, the Harvard Business School has built up quite a nice business licensing its case studies to other schools.)

Cases can range from half a page to more than forty pages. The shorter ones usually act as a starting point for discussion, while the longer ones can require detailed analyses. Often, professors will throw in "B" cases to spice things up. These are short addendums to the case—giving you more information, which may or may not change the way you think about your answer.

Case studies are known for their distinct lack of flair, style, and even grammar, for that matter. Behold, a typical opening: "Colford looked out of his office suite—everyone had gone home and he was left there by himself. He had the sales report on his desk. The next morning he would have to deliver his recommendation to the Board. He wondered what he would tell them . . . " What drama! What suspense! From there, it moves rather ploddingly into the details. You will soon notice that you get detail—sometimes a truckload of detail—on things that even for the sake of the simulation you couldn't care less about. This, while the information you really need is not readily accessible—instead, it is maddeningly spread out and offered in uneven formats (for example, sales could be in dollars for one year, in units for the next, and in yen for the one after that). The idea here is that, just like in the real world, you never have perfect information, and you have to screen out irrelevant noise. And it *is* noisy out there.

All of this is great in theory, and you'll definitely read a lot of valuable cases during the next couple of years. Unfortunately, there'll also be a lot of less-than-valuable cases, and plenty of painfully boring ones too. To counter this criticism, some schools have begun to overhaul the cases being used—sometimes writing new ones, in an effort to make these drills more relevant and useful. *Jungle* applauds this trend.

A WEEK IN THE LIFE OF AN MBA

Monday

7:00 A.M. Early workout at gym: stair machine, sit-ups, and bike.

8:20 A.M. Check e-mail.

8:30 A.M. Core class #1. Macroeconomics. Usually a lecture-style class.

10:00 A.M. Core class #2. Organizational Behavior—the introductory management course, in which you study how a company is organized, understanding the psychology of the workplace and personality types, profiles in corporate leadership, etc.

11:30 A.M. Meet with learning team for ten minutes after class to discuss plans for case due next week. Go to computer terminals to check e-mail, look at stocks, catch up on the latest e-businesses that have gone belly-up in last twenty-four hours.

12:15 P.M. Stop by management professor's office to set up lunch for next week. Take advantage of school program that pays for a few of these lunches every year. Stop by finance prof's office to sign up for office hours on Wednesday. Grab a sandwich, check voice mails, and return calls.

2:00 P.M. Core class #3. Finance. Heavy quant class and heavy workload, focusing on valuing companies and the cash flows behind them. Cold calling by professor.

4:00 P.M. Recruiting time. Go to career office to scour through files for informational-interview contacts. Do company research. Update resumé. Or if there is a presentation by a company you are interested in, attend and network.

6:00 P.M. Dinner with learning team on campus. Half hour of friendly chat slowly turns into two hours of debating case and number crunching, and planning who will do what in time for next meeting.

9:00 P.M.–midnight. Textbook and other assigned reading at home. Do problem set for Stats. Call friends.

Tuesday

8:00 A.M. Breakfast and *Wall Street Journal* at home. Put in a couple early calls to recruiting contacts. Remind self that they probably have caller ID.

10:00 A.M. Core class #4. Statistics. A grueling, number-crunching, and complicated course that serves as the basis for decisionmaking in all areas—from risk analysis to estimated values to population sampling.

11:45 A.M. Respond to e-mails, check stocks, news.

Noon. Club lunch meeting—finance, entrepreneurship, media/entertainment, marketing, etc. Guest speaker from the industry you want to work in. It's one part fun to two parts event planning and networking.

2:00 P.M. Core class #5. Corporate Strategy. Case-based class with heavy reading and learning teamwork required.

4:00 P.M. Class reading, review notes, start problem set for Macro, etc.

5:30 P.M. Attend on-campus lecture with visiting CEO. Usually popular events, for both students and professors. A great opportunity to see market movers speak unfiltered.

7:30 P.M. Dinner at home. Study. Finish problems for to-morrow's Macro class. Call Mom.

Late night. Complete problem set for finance class. Check in with Bill Maher or Dennis Miller. Read new issue of *MBA Jungle.*

Wednesday

7:30 A.M. Coffee with contact at a firm you are targeting for summer slot.

8:30 A.M. Core class #1. Macroeconomics.

10:00 A.M. Core class #2. Organizational behavior.

11:30 A.M. Go over class notes in coffee shop, check and return e-mail.

Noon. Brown-bag lunch meeting with club. Select and invite speaker for next event.

2:00 P.M. Core class #3. Finance.

3:30 P.M. Meet with professor after class.

5:00 P.M. Workout. Meet with classmate at gym for a game of squash and a weight workout.

7:00 P.M. Work on problem sets and reading.

8:30 P.M.–12:30 A.M. Learning team meeting. Integrate materials and further debate case. Much pizza and caffeine consumed. Split up to look up more information, then regroup to put the finishing touches on a great document.

Thursday

8:30 A.M. Coffee with second-year who summered at firm you're targeting for internship. Use his advice to update resumé, and prepare for first round interviews.

10:00 A.M. Core class #4. Statistics.

11:30 A.M. Review class notes, check e-mail, drop off laundry/dry cleaning.

Noon. Attend corporate presentation with friends. Much schmoozing and passing out of business cards. Meet contact you will call next week for coffee. Tuck away sandwich for consumption in next class.

2:00 P.M. Core class #5. Corporate Strategy.

3:30 P.M. Read case stuff for tomorrow's learning team meeting.

5:30 P.M. Enjoy a well-earned brew and blow off steam with your fellow students.

7:30 P.M. Go to Mexican restaurant with friends. Or Chinese. Or pan-Asian. Whatever. Just don't order the scallops.

Friday

7:30 A.M. Hit snooze button, sleep in a bit.

9:30 A.M. Tennis with classmates or run through campus.

Noon. Lunch meeting with learning team. Longer, more relaxed discussion, without the constraints of class, focusing on the major project due in a few weeks. First, the team debates the overall approach and strategy. The monster assignment is then broken up into manageable pieces, and three "subteams" of two, two, and one are assigned the three areas for next Friday's meeting.

4:00 P.M. Class reading, homework assignments.

6:30 P.M. Downtime, get ready for plans later on in the evening.

Saturday

10:00 A.M. Meet at school for a seminar on the informational interview: how to get them, who to get them with, and how to make them count.

Noon. Lunch with friends.

2:00 P.M. Career resource office and computer lab, tracking down information on targeted industry and learning more about specific firms within that industry.

5:00 P.M. Class reading, homework assignments.

9:00 P.M. Meet up with classmates/friends at restaurant to celebrate friend's birthday. Or some other real or made-up holiday. Remind self not to order the scallops.

Sunday

10:00 A.M. Downtime. No deliverables the entire day.

7:00 P.M. Start reviewing material for tomorrow's classes. Set up and organize for the coming week.

CHOOSING THE CURRICULUM:
ELECTIVES VERSUS THE CORE

Every school has a core group of classes that every student must take. You remember from college: The university wants to assure that its graduates are well-rounded, yada yada yada. Your business school makes a similar argument: It wants you to be well rounded on the various aspects of business. You may be a marketing whiz, but your school still wants you to be able to think intelligently about the macroeconomy. But I'm an adult, you say, and I can damn well make up my own mind about what courses I need. And let's not forget that I am paying 50 grand to be here. And isn't the point of going to business schools to focus on business? Specifically, the aspects of business I like and that can make me wildly successful and rich? Specifically, the ones that will allow me to crush all comers in the interview process and then again once I get the job? Well, yes, sort of.

Two things. First: When it comes to ensuring future success, the soft skills you learn are as important as the hard skills. You may be a hard-core banker, but sitting in an organizational behavior class and learning to deal with other nonbanking personalities will actually benefit your career. After all, you will have to deal with nonbanking types to succeed in the workplace. The second point is a bit less intuitive: You are training for your next job, yes, but you are also training for your *last* job. No, not the job you just left. Not your *previous* job. But the job you really *really* want to have in five or ten years. When you are CEO is not the ideal time to find yourself needing an intro to corporate strategy or an in-depth lesson on what debt ratio is. In fact, it is doubtful you can even make it to that point without some of those tools.

So there are actually very good reasons for having a core requirement—give these administrative guys *some* credit, they've been doing this for a while. Having said that, where you have some discretion to get out of a core class, do so. Say you have had accounting as an undergrad or have worked in accounting. There is no doubt that a refresher course will help you, but you can also brush up by spending a few hours with a textbook. By placing out of a core class, you can take an elective or more advanced class that will:

A. Be more interesting
B. Challenge you more
C. Be an opportunity to meet folks outside your bloc
D. Give you an edge

The answer is (e) all of the above.

What about that whole spiel of training for your last job? This is true, but placing out of a couple classes will not throw your career into hazy chaos. You will undoubtedly have other core classes that you must take, and that you would do well to take. And if you can manage to place out of organizational behavior, for instance, and take a more advanced management class, you get the benefits without the drawbacks.

Two big, fat, glaring exceptions to this rule. If the professor is supposed to be excellent, take the class. A great professor trumps every rule. Second, if the class is one of those formative, defining experiences that everyone talks about, you probably shouldn't miss it. And usually, it's a defining, formative class *because* the professor is a star. Bottom line: Unless you hear the professor is amazing, place out of the class if you can. That will be the right answer 90 percent of the time.

HOW TO SPOT A TOP PROF

Hey you. Yes, you. Wake up. You been paying attention? Good. Then you've pretty much figured out that you should find out who the great professors are and get into their courses. How important is this? On a scale of one to ten, yes, this one goes to eleven. It goes without saying that you will learn more and you will be inspired. But if you are lucky and good and maybe a little bit shrewd, you just might be able to befriend a start professor. That's a reward in and of itself. But it also might enable you to network with leaders in their fields. (More on this later.)

In some cases it will be obvious who the stars are—people will be buzzing about them. In other situations, though, you will have to dig. Most schools now have student ratings of a professor's past classes available on the Web or at the school's resource center. These can be enormously helpful—profs are rated in terms of their lecturing ability, the subject matter itself, and the workload they bestow upon their students.

Three Tricks for Prof-Hunting Season

1. Go to the videotape. Many schools tape lectures, as a courtesy to the students who have to miss a class. You can usually check these out of the library or watch them right there with headphones. This will pretty much tell you what you need to know.

2. Find a couple of second-years whom you respect. Ask them who *they* think the great profs are and push them for one that is not obvious. They will appreciate your interest in their opinions and may know something the other students are missing.

3. Sample the real thing. Go to meet the prof in person—a firsthand impression is invaluable. Not only that, but you will get a leg up in getting to know the professor, and that could be a good thing for class and beyond. Just introduce yourself (briefly) and ask about the themes of the class and his or her teaching style.

(Of course, the classroom is just the beginning. Did you ever stop to think that your professors represent one of the most powerful opportunities to network? See "Network with Professors—Without Kissing Up," Chapter 8.)

Don't be afraid to fight hard for the profs or the classes you want. You're investing your hard-earned money and, more important, your time in this experience. So do everything you can while more or less staying within ethical boundaries to make this happen. A great professor will make your return to the hallowed halls and classrooms an unforgettable experience.

7

The Learning Team— Like *Survivor,* but with Graph Paper

B-SCHOOL HAS CERTAIN SYSTEMS AND INFRASTRUCTURES THAT ONE MUST UNDERSTAND BEFORE THE FIRST DAY OF CLASSES. OTHERWISE, ONE WILL GO INTO CARDIAC ARREST UPON HEARING ABOUT CERTAIN ASPECTS OF THE EDUCATIONAL EXPERIENCE—SUCH AS LEARNING TEAMS.

Your learning team is the group of fellow students you will study with. Yes, you spend an ungodly amount of time with them. Yes, your grades depend on them. No, you can't choose who's on your team. This chapter will tell you how to escape with your sanity and transcript intact.

Of course, the tricky part is that the very qualities that make the greatest individual MBA students—ambition, brilliance, and a certain stubborn focus—can also make for the most dysfunctional learning groups. And you've got to learn to deal with it, because more and more schools have made teamwork an integral part of their curriculum.

Team learning isn't new to business schools, of course, but the big emphasis on group work is more evangelical than ever. A lot of the credit (or blame) should go to Donald Jacobs, longtime dean of Northwestern University's Kellogg Graduate School of Management. Back in the mid-1970s, he met

by Jeff Ousborne

with business leaders and hit upon the radical idea that future managers should learn to cooperate as well as compete.

Cooperation is one thing, but anyone who's ever hunkered down with a team knows how staggeringly inefficient groups can be. We're talking about the well-meaning guy who won't shut up about the three years he spent at J.P. Morgan. The erratic genius who can do elaborate decision trees in her sleep, but never learned the meaning of the word *plagiarism*. The slacker who hasn't shown up for a meeting in two weeks. The 2 A.M. argument with a former English major over where to put a semicolon. Then there's the whole notion of collective contribution, which can carry a touchy-feely taint, especially among hard-core quant jocks looking for ever-faster ways to calculate net present value.

Still, common sense suggests the value of collaboration: Not only are friendships (and future contacts) forged over the 3 A.M. coffeepot, but the nuances of an increasingly complicated business world often elude people who work exclusively in one area. On the other hand, the better you are at working with a team, the more effective and successful you will be with your career—no matter which profession you choose.

"It's systems theory: Cross-functional teams provide different viewpoints," says Margaret Neale, professor of organizations and dispute resolution at Stanford Business School. "You need as much complexity on a team as you have in the environment, because what looks like a marketing problem to one person may actually be more effectively considered as a finance problem when the entire group looks at it." Fred Talbott, a professor at Vanderbilt University's Owen Graduate School of Management, sees another payoff: "Managers in Western society spend 65 to 85 percent of their time listening," he says. "That means, in one sense, that you'll be getting paid 65 to 85 percent of your salary for listening. Group learning obviously encourages the habit."

It can also encourage a mean left hook or a head butt when time is short, tensions run high, and personalities begin to clash. There is some comfort, though, in the thought that whatever circle of hell you may find yourself in, somebody two years ahead of you has almost certainly suffered more—and still emerged with grades and career unscathed. But it goes beyond simple comfort. In the interests of efficiency, to say nothing of intrastudent bonhomie, it makes sense to learn from the mistakes of others, and to take any and all available shortcuts to team harmony.

As idiosyncratic as any individual team may be, most go through a series of predictable stages, known (in typically poetic B-school argot) as forming, storming, norming, and performing. And mercifully, there are strategies for negotiating each of them.

Forming: Of Quants and Kickball

A major factor in your experience will be whether teams are assigned or left for students to choose. In all likelihood, you'll be placed in a group during the first few days, if not pre-term. Most schools have developed elaborate systems for such assignments. Dartmouth's Tuck School is typical. "We think about what kinds of tasks a group is going to perform," says Associate Dean Ken Baker. "Then we look at what kinds of backgrounds students have, and spread them around to fertilize interaction." Even with the best of intentions, however, you can count on your team being at least somewhat random, and more often, completely so.

Less frequently, students will be allowed to choose their own teams. That's a mixed blessing, and, of course, a rare occurrence in the "real" business world—thus a school's reluctance to allow the practice. And counterintuitively, being able to select your own team does not guarantee a smooth process. "It can be a big nightmare," says Dave Tambling, a recent graduate of Duke's Fuqua School of Business. "You're in a class where you don't know anyone, and it's like the last five kids to get picked for kickball: 'Uh, I guess we're a group.'" For one econ course, he remembers, "The professor said, 'Don't team up with four engineers,' and we were like, 'Yeah, right,' and did it anyway to be sure everyone knew how to run spreadsheets. But we found that when you put four quant types together, they tend to be uptight and run things into the ground." As the year wears on, being able to look at problems from multiple points of view becomes increasingly important. So in picking your team, it makes sense to follow the rationale of those B-schools that make assignments: Try to be as well rounded as possible. If you don't, your group may end up like a squabbling, fourth-place baseball team with three all-star pitchers and a collective batting average of .188.

But just because one member of your splendidly diverse team claims to possess the precise skill needed for an assignment, don't bow down to the benevolent gods. In fact, it pays to beware the overconfident specialist—especially during the first month, when classmates are insecure and eager to impress. "I heard a story where there was a major assignment due, a big case involving an airline," says Chris Morris, a recent grad from the University of Rochester's Simon School of Business. "One person said, 'Oh, I worked for that company. Let me do most of this.' He showed up with a total piece of shit, and the team had to rewrite the report." The moral: Just because someone worked in marketing at Delta doesn't mean he's an expert on airline regulation.

As a team begins to take form, differences in job experience, academic interests, and cultural backgrounds start to matter far less than differing attitudes about the quality of work the group is going to produce. "Almost immediately, you see the biggest conflicts between those focused on getting the highest grades and those for whom it's just not a value," says Monica McGrath, Wharton's director of leadership and learning teams. Students who've been through it concur. "It's most important that you all agree on the level of effort you put in," says recent Duke grad Tambling. "I knew people who teamed up with a few drinking buddies, and only one of them really cared about doing good work."

The definition of good may vary from team to team; that's especially true at places like Harvard, where no recruiter will ever see your grades, or Carnegie Mellon, where there's no grade distribution curve. But either way, if you are talking about getting an A or a B or are concerned about the more intangible results of the work, it makes good sense to set expectations up-front—you will save yourself a lot of grief down the line. Generally, second-year students spend a lot less time obsessing over the difference between As and Bs and are much happier for it. Learn from them. According to Kerri Keisler, a 2000 grad from NYU's Stern School of Business, "Companies are hiring the whole package. They're looking at your leadership, your activities. Not a single recruiter asked about my grades."

When Teammates Attack!

Horror stories from group learning's dark underbelly:

Econ on the Rocks

We had a guy who'd frequently show up with his "dinner" in a paper bag from the liquor store. One night, he arrived having apparently had second and third helpings. It was clear that he hadn't read the assignment we were discussing. When I asked him, he slurred, "No, but I'm sure you guys can give me the highlights."

—SCOTT HORTON, Fordham University Graduate School of Business '00

Sweet Revenge

At one of our first study sessions, a woman arrived completely unprepared, and a guy in the group really let her have it. At the end of the term, the guy ended up writing the entire paper for the team. When he got a much lower grade on it than he'd expected, he questioned the instructor, who explained that one of

*his teammates had given him a poor participation grade. The
woman had gotten her revenge through peer voting.*

—KEITH WILCOX, Berkeley's Haas School of Business '01

All Dressed Up

*Late one evening at the end of the semester, a group member
presented some last-minute material for our project—which was
due the next day. It sounded a little too polished, and someone
asked if she had plagiarized the stuff. "No," she said cheerily. "I
got it for free from a Web site!" Then, at 2 a.m., she started
talking about her "vision" for the project. Later that morning—
mind you, it was now near dawn—she suggested that we coordi-
nate matching outfits for the big presentation.*

—JILL BATISTICK, Thunderbird Graduate School of
International Management '95

The Mother of All Teammates

*A man in my group flew in his mother to "take care of him" while
he was working on a big project. On the day she was to arrive, he
actually asked someone else in the group to pick her up. Two
weeks later he showed up without his part of the assignment. His
excuse was beautiful: He said his wife didn't have time to type it.*

—LAUREN SLEGONA,
Fordham University Graduate School of Business '02

Whatever It Takes

*It was our first semester, the time when everyone takes the in-
troductory course in management—how to work in groups,
team dynamics, that stuff. At the end of the term, each group
can vote to give up to two bonus points to a member they think
deserves extra credit—which can make a big difference in your
grade. Well, we decided as a group that no one would get the
bonus. But the guy we designated to turn in the final paper se-
cretly changed the vote and gave himself the two points. Did I
mention that he was a lawyer before he went to B-school?*

—ANONYMOUS, Wharton '97

Storming: I'm Okay, You're a Jerk

Sure, new acquaintances can be polite and solicitous. But in B-school, instant pressure (i.e., the first project) can mean instant trouble. That's deliberate. "Some groups are dealing with conflict on Day One. We're trying to get people to the point where they say, 'I don't know who the hell you are, you don't know who the hell I am, but we're going to make this work,'" says Joe Fox, associate dean of MBA programs at Washington University. "We're trying to accelerate that grudging acceptance of one another." The operative word is accelerate: In MBA programs, the normal growth of work relationships is squeezed into a dangerously short amount of time. Some teams have throw-downs within the first two weeks; but for most groups, conflict is less a matter of discreet shouting matches than it is of quiet tensions, nasty undercurrents, and loaded subtexts.

But here's the surprise: According to professors, if a group doesn't have these dynamics, it may not be performing well. "Part of the difficulty is that students can't distinguish between good conflict and bad conflict," says Stanford professor Neale, who, incidentally, used to be a marriage counselor. "There's relational conflict: 'I don't like you, you're weird,' which we want to minimize. And then there's task conflict, which has to do with having different ideas about how to get a job done. That's when you have a marketing person and an engineering person trying to solve a customer service problem. Occupational diversity doesn't have a positive effect until you have conflict like this." The opposing viewpoints of an ex-accountant and a former lawyer may actually be a group's greatest strength, because the best work is often done in the gaps between perspectives. Learning how to weather and thrive with these types of conflict is what it is all about.

Some clashes, of course, have less to do with past occupations than with personalities. And in the getting-to-know-you-really-really-fast storming phase, some personalities emerge right away. "One of the earliest problems teams face is the Dominator," says Anne Donnellon, an associate professor of management at Babson College and author of *Team Talk: The Power of Language and Team Dynamics.* "This person tends to direct. 'I'm going to do this, you're going to do that.' And that often leads to someone withdrawing from the group." Donnellon suggests that teams "create a process and assign a set of roles as early as possible. Give a quiet person a role that requires him to talk, like having him lead the discussion at the next meeting." If that doesn't work, try dealing with Dominators the way first-year HBS students do: They keep a stuffed shark around to toss at anyone who gets too overbearing.

The other *x* factor that teams have to come to terms with is gender. By all accounts, business school is the enemy of romance, probably because there's nothing less sexy than watching someone grind out a process flow diagram in a library study room. But subtle assumptions about men and women persist, and they can affect a group's work. "I have observed situations where it's assumed the woman will be the group's Peacemaker and secretary," says Donnellon. "Even worse, sometimes she accepts that role, no matter what her actual strengths are."

Still, theory about relational conflict is one thing; that total jackass sitting next to you is another. After a couple of months of stress and sleep deprivation, even a harmless-looking cost-accounting assignment can turn the most mild-mannered student into Travis Bickle. Vanderbilt graduate Sam Graber, a musician, watched his personality skirmishes with a teammate quickly escalate from angry e-mails to serious physical threats. Infuriating situations do arise, and having one difficult member can be like multiplying your group's collective potential by a fraction—or worse, by zero.

A team may need to save itself in extreme circumstances, even if that means doing something akin to amputation. Some groups have been known to approach the professor about kicking out a problem team member. "I saw one case where a student was so bad, contributed so little, so late, and so off the point that it seriously affected the group's grade," says Donnellon. "I have to admit that I've advised people, 'Look, you're just going to have to marginalize this person and minimize the damage.' Sometimes there's no choice." Besides bruised feelings and potentially tarnished grades, the biggest problem with such squabbles is opportunity cost. Every minute spent hurling insults is a minute lost forever.

Norming: A Toilet Full of Idealism

About halfway through the first term, when the work really heats up, a group's dynamic will start to resemble that moment when a well-designed backyard football play degenerates into everyone-run-around-until-someone-gets-open. But against that background of chaos, an interesting thing happens: All the personal politics and petty arguments fall to the side as the team rallies to conquer the task at hand. Some refer to this phenomenon as "norming." Others simply call it survival. "You come here with all these high ideals about really learning all the material for every project," says University of Rochester's Morris. "Then the work hits, all that goes down the toilet, and you start asking everyone, 'Okay, so what do you do best?'" Of course, if each team member focuses only on his area of expertise, nobody learns anything new. How much intellectual curiosity should be sacrificed on the altar of efficiency is a personal decision, but common sense dictates a few guidelines. Case discussions, for example, are great opportunities for everyone to have a say. But with more quantitative work, many teams find that it makes sense to rely on a member who's willing to lead everyone through the material. In many cases, a good compromise is to divide into subteams—where two people can tackle a specific issue—and that way you have the strength of someone who is already competent and someone who gets to tag along and learn more. The favor can be returned on the next assignment.

Perhaps the most difficult job is tackling a paper en masse, because writing by committee is inherently inefficient. "Doing a twenty-page paper is horrible," says Duke alum Tambling. "You spend tens of hours arguing over commas in the middle of the night; people get worn down and pissed off." Vanderbilt's Talbott offers a strategy: First, everyone in the group should brainstorm together, reaching for ideas without judgments. Then they should go back and make decisions about which ideas are actually worth keeping and how they contribute to the general shape and direction of the paper. Don't get sidetracked: "Keep your eyes on the prize," says Talbott. "If a professor says, 'You should cover x, y, and z,' then stay focused on that and nothing else." If the subsections are well delineated, you won't have a problem stitching the work together—one person should manage the task of transitions and basic fluidity. If the subjects are not as delineated, once everyone has put his or her piece in, find one person in the group who wants to take a stab at a first draft. "After you've got a draft, let one or two other people take a pass at it, just to make sure it's on track," adds Tiffany Breau-Metivier (Tuck '00). It's also a good idea to let everyone see the final version. "One group had an extremely difficult guy," says Morris. "He had one point of view; the rest of his team had another approach and voted to do the paper their way. But he volunteered to type it up—and he did it his way. They ended up getting a horrible grade."

Performing: The Promised Land

After nearly a year, after your eyes have gone squinty from lack of sleep, after you've fought off thoughts of frailty, failure, and homicide, you can expect another epiphany, a moment when the team shifts into overdrive and the engine purrs.

How will you know when your team is approaching its potential? Gaming—finding out what a professor wants on a paper or for the entire course—is an essential part of business school, and for effective groups, it becomes second nature. Even when it's insincere. "I've regurgitated stuff I completely disagree with, and it's worked perfectly," says Morris. Also, experienced teams spend as little time as possible on process. "At first, people love to talk and have meetings, and then have meetings about those meetings," says Christin Wingo, an MBA candidate at Vanderbilt. "Toward the end of the semester, we were spending much less time talking and more time actually doing things. You really see this in second-year groups."

Smart groups also worry less about grades. "First of all, the later you are into your MBA career, the less you are concerned about your grades," says one Columbia '01 student. But the big revelation is that by focusing on what is interesting and on delivering the best answer, the grades naturally follow.

"There's so much emphasis placed on numbers when you're applying to business school, it's natural to think they're important," says Fallaw Sowell, deputy dean of student and alumni affairs at Carnegie Mellon's Graduate School of Industrial Administration. "But during the job recruiting process, no one cares what your grades are. The emphasis is on deliverable skills. They're going to say, 'We've got this plant in Poughkeepsie with a problem. How would you handle it?'"

The final breakthrough is understanding that effective teamwork is all about knowing what you *don't* have to do. "There's no way you can accomplish everything," says Katie White (Kellogg '01). "Even in real business situations, you may have to make decisions without all the information you need. The trick is to remember the 80-20 rule." The notion that 20 percent of your business accounts for 80 percent of your profits is an important principle—and equally applicable to your B-school teamwork: Concentrate on the work that contributes the most to your grade. "When you get to 80 percent of the answer, you quickly hit diminishing returns," says one NYU prof who favors the case method. "Remember to focus on what's important—it may be time to move on to the next issue or problem." Or, as Graber puts it: "At first, if you had one little thing that didn't work, you'd stay up all night to fix it. Now you just say, 'Looks close enough to me. Let's go get some beer.'"

TEN WAYS TO ANNOY YOUR TEAMMATES

Because showing up late is so passé . . .

1. During meetings, dine from a plastic bag of clams.
2. Talk on your cell phone a lot. In an inexplicably thick Scottish accent. To the Dark Overlord.
3. If you are a guy, call all the women "doll-face" and "toots."
4. Insist on burning the edges to make your report look "really cool and old."
5. Use exclamation points in most of your sentences when writing reports.
6. Say "dot-com" after every sentence.
7. Repeatedly ask if they want to see your business plan for making left shoes.
8. Smoke from a long filtered cigarette.
9. Point out palindromes that aren't.
10. Insist on coming up with really cute names for your team. Suggestions: "The Busy Bees," "The Stat Pack," "Marshall."

by Justin Heimberg

HOW TO DEAL WITH TROUBLED TEAMMATES

The Dominator.   The Dominator always speaks first, according to Babson College professor Anne Donnellon, and takes up airtime that might otherwise be filled with someone else's good ideas. This person's a little like Eminem: annoying, but too good to ignore. Next time the Joker rebuffs a smart idea, call him on it. Otherwise he'll make others resentful and less willing to contribute.

The Joker.   The frequently deployed quips of the Joker can relieve the pressure of an all-nighter—or double it. Donnellon suggests keeping a close eye on the other team members' reactions: If the wisecracks and gags are too frequent or at all offensive, say so. If not, then, you know, go ahead and laugh.

The Wallflower.   Silent during meetings and reluctant to express ideas, Wallflowers are likely to feel alienated from the team, causing their productivity to suffer. Talking to Wallflowers one-on-one can make them more comfortable; and asking them to lead a meeting will give them a formal setting in which to share their ideas with the group.

The Peacemaker.   The Boutros Boutros-Ghali of the team, the Peacemaker smooths over potentially damaging fissures in the team's relationships. Which is great, as long as he or she doesn't smother the team into seamless agreement—skirmishes (also known as "productive conflict") often lead to good ideas.

8

The Recruiting Game: Building the Network

··

THE DIRECTOR OF CAREER DEVELOPMENT AT A LEADING MBA PROGRAM ONCE ADDRESSED AN AUDITORIUM FULL OF EAGER FIRST-YEAR STU-DENTS WITH THE FOLLOWING ADMONITION: "STUDY HARD, BUT DON'T forget the *real* reason you are in business school." Of course, she was speaking tongue-in-cheek, but there's a great deal of truth to the notion that one of the most important reasons for going to B-school in the first place is the bundle of opportunities that can await you at the finish line.

At the very beginning, most people find competing for a job a bit of a weird experience. For starters, it can be jarring to realize how soon after you begin classes you actually have to start thinking about getting your resumé together. And networking. And going to company presentations. You have to get comfortable talking about yourself—even bragging about yourself—and telling your "story" to recruiters. And you have to do this to a degree you never had to—or wanted to—before. And then you have to remember to "turn it off" again when you are out with friends and family. And, of course, you must drill yourself until your interviewing skills are honed to a razor-sharp edge.

NETWORKING: WINNING STRATEGIES

The best jobs are never advertised in the papers. The lucrative deals aren't posted on the Web. It's all about connections. And everyone you know—from your first-grade teacher to the guy who snored his way through Stats 101 to Sammy "Knuckles" D'Agostino—is a potential resource. The good news: There's no finer place to network than B-school. Here's how to begin the drill and make it pay off.

Basic Training

Let's start with the basics: your friends and family. It is definitely worthwhile to make a list of all of your friends, your family, your family's friends, and so on and include their company and industry. Yes, yes, this sounds positively moronic. Yes, yes, it sounds like the kind of hooey that a peppy "guidance counselor" might sling your way. But once it's all committed to paper, everyone is surprised by the network they already have. So just suck it up and go through the exercise. You can thank us later.

Your first step: Write a letter to friends/contacts that explains your situation, what job(s) you are looking for, and why you think you are an attractive candidate. The idea here is simply to provide them with an update on any recent developments in your life (e.g., attending Sam's Backyard B-school), as well as your plans for the future. This little update/reminder allows them to pause, let their wheels spin a bit, and ponder whether they or someone they know might be helpful in your job search. The trick here is to provide your contacts with ammunition so that they can be effective agents for you. Give them the sound bite they need. If you'd like them to call down to their HR department and say, "Stephanie has a strong quantitative background as well as international experience relevant to our business," then use those words in your letter. If you don't provide solid specifics about your plans and goals, your contact will call the HR guy and mutter something about "the daughter of a friend who's supposed to be smart and makes a mean margarita."

E-mail is also a good vehicle for this type of networking: you get a quick response, and your note is easily forwardable to others in the network. Should one of your friends give you another contact of theirs whom you don't know, definitely follow it up, no matter how lame or half-baked the connection might appear. Why? (1) If you don't, you make your friend look bad; (2) your friend probably wouldn't have suggested the person if she believed it was a dead end; (3) it's a great opportunity to break out of your direct network; and (4) that person may know someone really good for you to meet. Also, even if the contact doesn't pay off in terms of an immediate job offer, you're building a network for your future, and this will pay handsome dividends.

> HINT FROM HELOISE.   Make sure you update your friends as to what came of their contacts, and thank them for their efforts. This is good manners, to be sure, but it also provides positive reinforcement for them, and they are more likely to give you another contact in the future.

The Squeaky Wheel . . .

When it comes to networking, you can be whatever dwarf you want to be as long as it isn't Bashful. If you're under the impression that asking someone for a contact is violating some kind of protocol, well, you would be incorrect. You have to ask politely. You have to respect any person's decision not to pass you along—"no" is an answer, too. But any fears about "stepping over the line" are misplaced. Think about it like this: Most firms, especially the elite firms, spend enormous amounts of time, thought, and money to target the best and the brightest. If you're a good fit for one of these firms and someone you know can make an introduction, they'll be doing that firm a great service. Their stock in the company will soar. You have to remember that people may help you for any number of reasons, not just out of the goodness of their heart. They may even welcome the opportunity—call it enlightened self-interest.

Still, many have hesitations. "Should I ask my father's accountant if he knows anyone in asset management?" A good rule of thumb is to put yourself in that person's shoes. Would you be put off if a someone you knew sent you a note with your qualifications and asked you if you knew anyone in their field they could speak with? Most likely you would be happy to help.

A certain number of students subscribe to the do-it-yourself philosophy. You know, the "I want to get this job on my own, without any help" types. If you fall into this camp, we've got a little news flash for you: The most a referral will ever do for you is get you an interview. From then on, you're on your own. Rest assured, if you get the offer, you will have done so on your merits, and on your merits alone.

Look to Your Left and Right

Could there be a better place to network than business school? Resources are everywhere, and everybody wants information. Your best resources are your fellow students. Think about it: If you were to imagine the ideal contact, it would be someone who knows the right people, someone with credibility, someone who's been in your shoes, someone who can offer solid advice. Second-year students fit this bill perfectly. Most firms specifically encourage their summer associates to report back to them about which first-years are worth talking to. Again, this makes perfect sense—top firms want top people—and who better than people they know on campus to act as conduits? In time, students in your own year will be of even greater help to you (more on that later), but for the jobs you want now, second-years are your best option—and one that often goes overlooked.

How to do it: You won't have many—if any—classes with second-years, but there are ways to increase your contact with these walking resource guides. Becoming involved with a club is perhaps the best action plan. Joining a club enriches your B-school experience anyway—many companies, for instance, give consideration to club members, it helps you focus your interests, and you meet people with whom you have something in common. The "people" who run the clubs are usually second-years. They will already have met people in the industry and all sorts of people who can help you. And who want to help you.

Once you have developed a relationship, it is perfectly acceptable to have a coffee with a second-year or a teacher's assistant (another great and often untapped resource) to discuss career issues. Do your homework. You don't want to say to the second-year who interned at Salomon Smith Barney: "Well, I can't really make up my mind between banking, consulting, and sales & trading." This is no time for soul-searching. Instead, you want to show that you know something about the industry and are smart and thorough. Don't forget: People who recommend you to their employers have put their own reputation on the line—they will never recommend someone they think will make them look bad. Once they feel comfortable—and that may take more than one double-skim extrafoam cappuccino—most second-years will have no problem recommending you for a company's interview list or giving you the name of someone at the company who can put you on the list.

INSIDER TIP.

- Meet as many second-years as you can, of course, but also make a special effort to identify the second-years who worked at the firms you want to work for.
- Befriend them early in the semester, but before you start plugging them for info and contacts, definitely wait until after their own interview process is near completion (which is before first-year interviewing starts). They will know you better and will also be over a good deal of the

pressure from their own interviewing, and they will simply know more. If they have already accepted an offer, or you feel you know them well enough, give it a whirl.

- Don't—don't! don't!—be one of the people who sends an e-mail like this: "Dear Ted, I am a first-year at Darden, and I heard you interned at Booz Allen. I am interested in working there—could you send me your contacts so that I could send them my resumé." Believe it or not, people coming back from internships get these all the time and the reaction is uniformly negative. It is also accompanied by a swift depression of the "delete" key. The take-away: Networking is about exchange; you have to give to get, even if the only thing you have to give is coffee, donuts, and a couple of knock-knock jokes.

School Ties

Your business school also has great institutional resources for networking. Aside from your fellow students and professors, it offers students an implicit promise that along with their sheepskin, they will have access to a network of distinguished graduates.

Most schools have a database of alums, sorted conveniently by graduation year and industry. Sound like a gold mine? It is. But you have to play by the rules. The alums have agreed to list their name and contact info on the condition that it not be abused. So your career resource center most likely has strict guidelines on how many names you can pull and how often any one name can be called.

HINT. Go to the career office early and start looking at names. Even if you don't call them right away, at least you'll have them and you won't have to fight the crowds later to get them. Also, it can often take weeks to set up a time to talk, and you have a distinct advantage if you're the first to call a contact rather than the seventeenth to ask for an informational interview.

Once you have identified the area(s) you want to focus on, go to the database and pull the relevant names. In some cases, the school will call the alum with a heads-up to say you'll be getting in touch. When you get your contact on the phone, say you are a current student at The School of Angry Tuna, looking to learn about, say, the marketing industry, and more specifically about Johnson & Johnson's program. Unless there are extenuating circumstances, you should be able to land an informational interview, if not in person then at least by phone.

You can take advantage of school ties even if the person has not registered on the database. Call or e-mail the person, and respectfully take your best shot. Sometimes, you'll get an opening. For most alums, fondness for an alma mater increases in proportion to their success. Of course, this isn't always the case, but it is worth a try, especially if your contact list for your target industry is otherwise thin.

> **INSIDER TIP.** An initial e-mail should be brief and to the point: Explain why you're contacting the person, what you're looking for, and how he can help you. It's a good idea to include a compelling subject line that will convince the person to open your message. "Referred by _____" or "Fellow alum looking for help" are two good bets. Later, when you reach the person by phone, your call will be expected, and your contact will be better prepared to help you.

By the way, your undergraduate institution can also be a tremendous help. It, too, has a sparkling database organized by class and industry.

Following Up

Follow-up doesn't have to be elaborate, but it distinguishes the best networkers from the pack. Since potential contacts have their own network of friends and colleagues, it is important that your name be the one that comes to mind when they hear of suitable job openings.

Ensuring that your name (and the favorable impression you've created) stays at the top of your contact's mind is something you should set in motion as soon as you've finished your first phone chat or meeting. Start with an immediate follow-up e-mail—something like "nice to meet you" is fine, but it is even better if you can add a line or two that will remind the person of your discussion. In today's digital world, where everyone communicates by e-mail, a handwritten note will really make you stand out. You can also show your interest in the company you want to work for by reading and clipping relevant articles. Send them to your contact with a few of your thoughts or just a note saying you thought he would enjoy the clip.

> **INSIDER TIP.** Maintain a networking "log book" of all of your contacts and the date on which you last contacted them. This will keep you up-to-date and will prevent the disastrous "you just called me last week" scenario.

NETWORK WITH PROFESSORS—
WITHOUT KISSING UP

Behold networking's holy grail. Their advice is good. Their contacts are better. Hell, they might even help you get rich.

When Adele Oliva was gunning for a prestigious Kauffman Fellowship four years after B-school, a recommendation from David BenDaniel, a former professor of hers at Cornell's Johnson School of Management, helped seal the deal. Ben-Daniel also helped Oliva get her foot in the door at Patricof & Co., a hot New York VC firm, where Oliva is now a partner. "Looking back," she says, "I wouldn't be where I am if it weren't for David."

---

by Jeff Ousborne

The lesson is as plain as the digits on Oliva's paycheck: Professors are among the most crucial career resources a student can cultivate. And an introduction to a future employer is only the beginning. Professors can provide insight on starting a business, connecting to venture capitalists, even solving problems at work. But they can't—and won't—go the extra mile for everyone. So how best to distinguish yourself? How to develop a lasting relationship? And thorniest of all, how to accomplish this without shamelessly sucking up (a strategy that will likely backfire, not to mention shrivel your soul)?

Fork Over the Insights

Got a few pearls of wisdom on niche marketing from your brand-management stint at P&G? Share it in class. Professors have a near-bottomless appetite for real-world anecdotes (good stories are hard to come by, and no teaching tool is more powerful). "Having worked five years at Microsoft before business school is valuable experience to a teacher who's been in academia all his life," says David Downes, director of the MBA program at UC–Berkeley's Haas School of Business. (Downes's comment, by the way, reflects a key principle for establishing a good relationship with professors: You scratch their back, they'll scratch yours.) If the anecdote plays well, and if you really want the teacher to remember you, consider providing him or her with a contact inside your former firm; the teacher might want to pursue it further sometime.

A few words about the anecdotes themselves: Keep them relevant (gratuitously dropping the name of a former firm is obnoxious), don't offer a story for every occasion (nobody likes a know-it-all), and be public-spirited. "Don't bring me an anecdote after class that would have been helpful to the entire group," says Jay Barney, director of Ohio State's Fisher School of Business. "I'd much rather you share it."

Dodge, Thrust, Parry

Professors are professional intellectuals, which means they welcome a good debate. Seth Goldman, a 1995 graduate of the Yale School of Management, regularly challenged the thinking of his competitive-strategy professor, Barry Nalebuff. The habit, Goldman says, made a lasting impression ("He liked that I turned the tables when not many others did"), and it paid big dividends.

A few years after Goldman graduated, he wanted to start his own soft-drink business, so he contacted his former teacher for advice. The two wound up going into business together, and today Honest Tea is a multi-million-dollar brand. "Don't be contentious for the sake of it," says Nalebuff. "But if you have a counterpoint, don't be afraid to offer it." A student hardly looks like a kiss-up when she openly disagrees with the professor.

Upsize Your Relationship

If you want to be a teaching assistant, you should approach the professor on the first day of class, right? Wrong. Get to him a week before classes start. Wait. Get to her the prior semester. Even if the professor can't use you that term, he will certainly remember your enthusiasm, which could win you the post the next time around (that's exactly what happened to Adele Oliva). Regular contact with a good instructor is the obvious attraction of being a TA; the bonus is that a bond often develops when two people work together to eviscerate—er, evaluate—other students' work.

Helping a professor with research is another way to forge closer ties. "There's a lot of boring stuff that needs to be done—coding data, going to the library," says Ohio State's Jay Barney. "But do it well and you become part of his team."

Know Your Target

Not interested in doing research or being a TA? Simply providing a newspaper clipping that's pertinent to a professor's research, class discussions, or private-sector interests can set one student apart from the rest (provided it's not from that day's *Wall Street Journal*, which is probably already dog-eared on the prof's desk). An Internet search makes finding professors' private-sector interests easy; if nothing else, profs will be impressed that a student bothered to learn more about their work.

Initiate Contact

If it weren't for all the other students lined up outside the door, a professor's office hours might seem the perfect time to establish a connection. Thus, these tips: Arrive before the throngs. (The professor will be more focused on you.) Ask questions rather than demand answers. ("Don't act as if it's the professor's duty to help," says Elaine Hagan, associate director of entrepreneurial studies at UCLA's Anderson School of Management. "It's a turnoff.") Get to know a professor's assistants—and call them by name. (It's an excellent way to get access if the professor is always booked or "in a meeting," says Downes, from Berkeley's Haas School.) And if you want career-related advice during office hours, don't pretend you're there to discuss nuances of the Capital Asset Pricing Model. "Just say what you want," explains Richard Freedman, a professor at NYU Stern. "A little shamelessness is fine."

Sweeten the Pot

Another approach is to become active in a club—investment banking, entrepreneurship, whatever your interest—then plan to ask a professor to speak at an event (he'll be flattered). If the professor can't make it, display his name as a distinguished invitee on the club web site or promotional materials, then let the professor know about it (people love seeing their names in print). A more subtle trick: Have a first-year student introduce himself to a professor and mention that you recommended him.

But don't limit the networking to the campus directory. Students can expand their Rolodex by tracking down a professor at another school. What Asian-currency-derivatives specialist wouldn't be impressed that a student from a different school has taken the initiative to seek her out?

SIX WAYS *NOT* TO IMPRESS A PROF

1. Whittle feverishly during class. If professor inquires about your peculiar habit, remark, "Sure, laugh now, but when they come, I'll be ready."

2. Answer professor's cold calls by verbalizing your entire thought process as if you were on *Who Wants to Be a Millionaire.*

3. Wear black turtleneck and beret to class; snap fingers rhythmically and say, "Save me the lecture, Daddy-o. We don't need this whole square vibe you're giving off."

4. Measure self against classroom wall every day, marking a line of chalk over your head. Get increasingly upset at your "lack of personal growth."

5. Stand up in middle of lecture. Tell professor that you are East Coast B-school, and you don't like what he's been saying about your boys.

6. Purposely answer a question incorrectly in front of the class. Then whimper, "This is the worst birthday ever!"

by Justin Heimberg

Plan It

Although few people actually go into business with a professor, working on a business plan together is a great way to network. It's an opportunity to demonstrate smarts, ambition, and commitment—and, of course, professors will be flattered that you sought out their wisdom.

Most students go about this gambit incorrectly: They present the professor with a fully formed plan and ask for feedback. Instead, run the idea past the professor in summary form first. A solid, well-outlined idea may pique interest. As it develops, send updates by e-mail. It doesn't require much effort on the professor's part to follow your progress—and it lends insight into how you think. Who knows? Your professor may be so dazzled that he'll say those magic words: "I'm impressed by your work. I've got a friend I'd like you to meet."

WHY YOUR RESUMÉ GOT TOSSED—AND WHAT YOU COULD HAVE DONE TO PREVENT IT

The average recruiter sees 5,000 resumés a year. Any legitimate reason she finds to make one disappear makes her life that much easier—and yours that much harder. Here, top-level recruiters reveal how candidates blow their chance to get a foot in the door.

The Numbers Don't Add Up. If accomplishments can be quantified, do it—but use discretion. Brandishing borderline performance numbers signals a lack of experience and bad judgment. "Phrases like 'Managed a budget of $500,000' or 'Led a team of two' might catch my eye in a bad way," warns Olaf Weckesser, who recruits for McKinsey & Co. Better to spin it as "Managed company's largest budget." Adds Alexandra DeMarino, a Citigroup recruiter: "If a small number is impressive, you absolutely have to put it in context." Because

by Sara Goldsmith

you can't provide context for academic numbers, don't include GMAT scores below 650 if you're targeting a top firm. DeMarino suggests bragging about nothing less than a 3.7 GPA.

Formality Takes a Vacation.   Don't succumb to the informality of e-mail. "If you send a cover letter by e-mail that starts with 'Hi,' it and your resumé will probably end up in the trash," says Cynthia Shore, assistant dean at the University of Buffalo's School of Management and director of its career-resource center. Treat an e-mail as you would a proper letter: Instead of "Hi," write "Dear Mr. Case." Instead of "Thanks," conclude with "Sincerely."

Keywords Are Overused.   It's true that recruiters sometimes use scanners to sort through resumés looking for certain keywords. But resumés appear contrived when candidates consciously try to include them. Describing a business-development position using such terms as "needs assessment" and "contract analysis" in order to squeeze in more keywords is a misguided strategy. Assume that a person—not a computer—will be reading the resumé. After all, fewer than 25 percent of recruiters even use scanners.

Things Get Too Personal.   "If you mention your age, we have to trash your resumé," says Jeremy Eskenazi, vice president of talent acquisition at Idealab!, the California incubator firm. Since it's illegal for a company to solicit a candidate's age, race, or marital status during the hiring process, firms have adopted a "don't tell" policy to avoid potential bias suits. Many won't risk even having it handed to them.

It Looks Too Fancy.   "A recruiter who receives resumés in pretty plastic folders will likely toss them," says Dave Opton, former VP of personnel for Sterling Drug International. "I just don't have time to take the damn things apart." Another faux pas: folding a resumé so that it fits into a standard business envelope. Heavy-stock paper that retains its crease can be a nuisance. Says Opton: "They're easier to store and photocopy if they're flat." Also, don't try to differentiate your resumé with boxes, bars, or ornate lettering. When recruiters see a resumé that's designed differently, they think the person's trying to hide something. Instead, focus on content and your resumé will rise to the top of the pile.

LEAVING THE PERFECT VOICE-MAIL MESSAGE

Interviewing is an art. Resumé writing is a science. And leaving a bad voice-mail on a recruiter's answering machine is the kiss of death. Here's why executives delete voice-mail messages—and how to make sure yours won't be one of them.

Hi, Ms. Stevens. It's Robert. Just a few thoughts on this guy's proposal. It's kind of like the problem we had back in March. Am I making myself clear? Well, I just think . . .

How important is an effective voice-mail? Put it this way: According to a study conducted by Pitney Bowes, the typical office executive receives upward of 375 communiqués every day, including e-mails, phone calls, faxes, and letters. In this environment, any excuse that a caller gives an exec to delete a voice-mail—even five slightly rambling seconds—is a valid one.

Start Strong

The single worst thing to do is to clutter the beginning of a message with useless information (phone-tag jokes most certainly qualify). According to Jacqueline Whitmore, founder of the Protocol School of Palm Beach, Florida, the superfluous pleasantries so many people rely on to start their messages

by Paul Scott

make a distinctly negative impression on busy executives. "Don't say 'I hope you're having a good day,'" she explains. "That's a cliché that doesn't mean anything." Instead, signal that you won't waste the person's time—state your name, reason for calling, and phone number up front. Keep your message to less than thirty seconds and you come off as someone who takes action rather than someone who talks about it.

Give 'em Structure

If there are several items of business to address, announce them right away, and then take each in turn. "There's a structure to all communications that linguists refer to as the frame, the context in which people expect to hear certain things," says Suzette Haden Elgin, associate professor emeritus of linguistics at San Diego State University. "Anything that breaks people out of the frame causes them to start missing the information." Nail the structure of the message by taking sixty seconds before you call to scratch out four or five bullet points. Yes, it sounds simplistic, but it can mean the difference between a lucid message and a meandering mess. It also drastically reduces the "ums" and "ers" that signal nervousness and lack of professionalism.

Pace Yourself

In making snap judgments about which messages to attend to, people often unconsciously take linguistic cues from the caller's delivery. Speaking too slowly could mean the beginning of a long, drawn-out voice-mail. Speaking too fast forces the listener to replay the message, or, more likely, to move on to the next one. Subtle phrasing can also send unwanted signals. "Women in particular often lift their intonation at the end of a sentence, as you would for a question," says Erin McKean, who edits *Verbatim*, an academic journal about language. "That can make you sound tentative and hesitant."

Say It Again

Repeat your phone number at the end of the message, and when you do, break it into groups of three or four digits. "Linguistic studies have proven that people tend to remember information more accurately when it's delivered in short chunks," says Elgin. "That's why they originally decided to group phone numbers into distinct clumps."

Get Technical

Digital voice-recording systems are designed not to capture silence. "A soft, barely audible word can be mistaken for silence and not preserved in a message," says Seth Munter, manager of technical training at Siebel Systems in San Mateo, California. Many systems also offer "flags" to mark a message as urgent and move it to the front of the line. (Less than 1 percent of callers take advantage of this function.) While doing so might make you look a bit pushy, it certainly demonstrates a facility with technology and a distinct by-any-means-necessary attitude.

9

Mastering the Interview

···

THE INTERVIEW

What does all your diligent networking and sterling resumé get you? An interview with a prospective employer . . .

Landing the interview is like getting a callback for a movie audition: The job isn't yours yet, but you have made it through the first of many contests. You're very much in the game. It's the first yardstick of success as you make your way through the recruiting landscape. There are generally three types of interview appointments: closed list, open list, and no list.

Closed list is the standard at most schools. Basically, you submit your resumé, cover letter, blood type, and the rest, and that, along with any good impressions you have made in person or through contacts, gets you on a select, invite-only list of people the firm in question wants to talk to.

An *open list* is when a firm tells your school they want to interview, say, twenty students, and they don't care who they are. The school then opens up those slots to students in a bidding/auction process—each student has so many points and can bid on so many slots offered by so many different companies. Generally, firms prefer closed lists (because they get to prescreen students) and schools prefer open lists (because they get to proclaim that *all* their students are great and also get to give "wild-card" opportunities to students). Firms generally get their way, so you will usually find either a closed list for a firm or a combination closed-open list, where some slots are allocated for auction.

No list is, well, no list. Neat, isn't it? The firm in question does not have a relationship with your school. This is less common, but still happens because many firms only recruit at programs that meet their ranking or geographic or other criteria. You can still get interviewed at a given firm, you just have to work a bit outside the normal system. In fact, many school-firm relationships were started because one student fought her way in, and the next year the firm wanted to look at other students from that school.

When does all this happen? Many schools have a set-aside period specifically for interviewing, and all firms are asked to conduct interviews during that time. There is very definitely an interview season—you'll know it by the nice clothes people wear, not to mention the freshly clipped hair and the preponderance of stress in the air. Folks will be cramming for interviews, studying information about the companies and industries, and brushing up on interview skills. There's also a fair bit of gossip—who got on what list, who got negged, and who got passed to the next round. The stakes are high, and the tone is all business as you set out to compete with the best and brightest for some of the sweetest job offers in the land.

The first round of interviews is generally done on campus or at a nearby hotel or other facility. Basically, a very simple room, your interviewer, and you. If you pass muster, you will be asked to interview for a second round—and sometimes more after that, depending on the firm. The latter rounds are generally done at the firm, and the format can vary: Some firms put two interviewers in the same room with one candidate, and others interview multiple candidates in a group setting.

INTERVIEW QUESTIONS:
INSIDE THE MIND OF A RECRUITER

You've prepared for the questions, of course. Done the mock interviews. Practiced your rap in the mirror. But then all of a sudden it's show time: Your audience is a recruiter, and every answer is your final answer. So what's a recruiter looking for in a response? We popped eight typical interview questions to a dozen MBA candidates, and then let our expert panel dissect the answers.

The *Jungle* Panel

Dianne DeSevo is the recruiting manager for Warner Music Group, which hires for Elektra and Atlantic, among others. Previously, she was a recruiter for HBO.

Todd Hutchings is a former recruiter for Internet consulting firm MarchFirst. During the 2000 recruiting season, he typically interviewed 300 candidates.

Rebecca Butler, the MBA recruiter for UBS Warburg investment banking, has screened hundreds of candidates over the last three years.

Jeannie Yang, a staffing consultant for Inktomi, screens every candidate for the marketing side of this Internet-infrastructure software company.

Where do you see yourself in five years?

I hope to be a key member of your management team. Having worked five hard years making great contributions to this company, I will have become one of its leaders. I'd be thinking of ways to grow the company and finding good people to bring in.
                    —*Second-year student, management consulting*

DIANNE DESEVO: I hate it when someone says, "I want to be in an executive position," because it doesn't talk about how you plan to get there. You need to discuss learning specific skills and networking. That's what shows me you have a real plan.

TODD HUTCHINGS: This is a canned line if I've ever heard one. It's more appropriate to talk about what you hope to become—you know, "I hope to develop customer-relationship management expertise." Personal accomplishments are what attract me to a candidate.

REBECCA BUTLER: I want to hear about where you want to be in terms of yourself rather than your position in my company. Talk to me about things you want to conquer, personality traits you want to improve.

Describe a bad decision you made.

Okay, here's one: When I was sixteen years old, I worked at a little neighborhood store. My friend was working there with me, and after a few weeks she got fired. The next day, out of loyalty to her, I quit. Poor decision. But I learned from that: Now I separate business from pleasure. When I'm at work, it's a professional environment and I don't take things personally.
—*Second-year student, media and entertainment*

HUTCHINGS: How about something from the recent past? We all make mistakes, and she should be big enough to discuss an error that she made recently.

BUTLER: She should have started her response with the lesson learned: that she knows how to separate business from pleasure. A recruiter's attention span can be short, and it's important that you capture my interest immediately.

DESEVO: This shows loyalty to a friend, which is a plus. I like that she looks over the whole of her life and learns from it. That said, I would have prefaced the answer with "I can give you a more current answer, but here's one that really stuck with me."

What's your greatest weakness?

I could give you the canned answer, but you probably don't want to hear that. I guess the thing I need to work on is prioritizing. I like doing many projects at once, and I sometimes focus on the things I enjoy doing rather than on the things that I should be doing.

—*Recent graduate, business development*

BUTLER: I'd be curious to know what you think it is I don't want to hear. Don't tempt me.

DESEVO: I don't love the "canned answer" part because it's almost mocking the question. And when you answer with "I'm a perfectionist" or "I take on too much," you're telling me that you're more interested in putting a positive spin on the question than you are with being honest. Just tell me a real weakness. That insight is worth something to me. This morning someone said, "I'm very sensitive; I have a hard time taking negative feedback." That's a good, honest answer.

JEANNIE YANG: I think this is a valid response. I'm looking for someone who knows herself, someone who knows her limitations, and plans to better herself.

HUTCHINGS: I like it. Because one thing it takes to succeed is the ability to decide between what's urgent and what's important.

Tell me about a challenge you faced and how you overcame it.

When I first started working, I wasn't technically savvy. I always figured computers would get easier to use. Eventually I realized that if I didn't figure this stuff out, I'd sink. I made a concerted effort to learn different software apps—Word, Excel, PowerPoint, and others. I read up on operating systems and processing speeds. It was a fair amount of effort, but I've gone from being a guy who knew nothing to the one people turn to for help.

—*Second-year student, financial analysis*

HUTCHINGS: Good answer. It shows, in detail, how he took initiative and masterfully addressed a skill gap. That said, I'd ask a follow-up question: "Hey, I'm having a problem with my computer, can you show me how to fix it?" That will quickly show me if he's for real.

BUTLER: Addressing technology is a good way to answer this kind of question, because technology will continue to pose a challenge for everyone. Ideally, I'd like to hear how he applies that lesson elsewhere and prevents the same sort of thing from happening in the future.

DESEVO: Perfect. It highlights a hard-core skill he brings to the table, as well as the willingness and ability to learn. He could talk a bit more about the way he learned—classes, networking, whatever—because that shows how he solved the problem. I love to hear about networking and building relationships. I always look for that.

What would you do if you didn't get this position?

First of all, I really want this position. I think I can be a tremendous value to this firm. I don't know if I should say this or not, but I have interviews with other companies, and I'm confident that I'm going to get a good offer from someone.

—*Second-year student, equity analysis*

YANG: This feels like a threat. It's good to be confident, but I don't like a candidate bringing up other companies if I don't specifically ask. You're here to talk about us, not about them.

DESEVO: I agree, but these days, it's a candidate's marketplace. So I buy that line.

How many gas stations are there in the continental United States?

Gas stations? In the U.S.? There's never one when you need one, I know that. May I use a pen and paper? Well, I'd figure out how many people drive cars. How many go to a gas station in a day? How many are there? I'd say 150,000.

—*First-year student, investment banking*

BUTLER: This type of question shows me how you'd handle yourself in front of a client, so the humor may not be appropriate. I'm looking at your body language—do you run your hand through your hair, roll up your sleeves?—and I'm listening for the first thing that comes out of your mouth, because I want to see how you deal with being put on the spot.

HUTCHINGS: With a case interview question, you're looking for the candidate to demonstrate comfort with numbers and analytic reasoning. This answer is not detailed enough. There are a few ways to skin a cat, and you should mention all of them, then dig deeper into one and show me that you can handle it. Here, the process is more important than the actual number.

DeSEVO: In my field, I look for creativity more than analytic skills. So I'll ask a question like "How do you find a needle in a haystack?" The best answer I've heard was "I'd burn the haystack."

Tell me about a situation in which you disagreed with a superior and how you handled it.

Well, I try not to disagree with my superiors, but it happens in the course of a dynamic working relationship. Once, we had to do a presentation for some regular clients. My boss wanted to go the formal route with slides. I wanted to talk to them, not speak at them. He won, he got his way.

—*Second-year student, brand management*

HUTCHINGS: He didn't really answer the question. So I'd ask it again. A good answer would be something like "I did my homework and brought the relevant facts—such as *x*, *y*, *z*—to the table and convinced my boss beyond a reasonable doubt."

YANG: Too vague. And he didn't really *handle* it, did he?

DESEVO: To say "he got his way" sounds catty and immature.

FOUR KILLER QUESTIONS

Pro bowlers have a beloved ball. Rock stars have their go-to axe. And recruiters? They have a favorite question, the one they trust to elicit the best information. Four to chew on.

1. What did you hope to get out of your previous job that you didn't?
   —REBECCA BUTLER

2. How do you handle somebody you work with who doesn't care for you?
   —DIANNE DESEVO

3. What would you tell me about yourself that would make you memorable to me?
   —JEANNIE YANG

4. How do your parents describe you?
   —TODD HUTCHINGS

What would you rather be doing right now?

Interesting question. With all due respect, I would like to be out in front of this building, as if it were an hour from now. That way this interview would be over, and hopefully I would have impressed you enough that I'd have this job.

—*First-year student, marketing*

YANG: I could have conjured up this answer, which doesn't impress me.

DeSEVO: First, recruiters don't want your feedback about what you thought of their question. This particular question is one recruiters use to get you to let down your guard. People tend to say something like "lying on a beach," but that's got nothing to do with why I would hire you. The trick is to stay focused. For me, a good answer would be something job related—like reading *Billboard* magazine, or thinking up ways to put Napster out of business.

Speak No Evil!

In a job interview, your body language speaks volumes to a recruiter.

In all likelihood, a recruiter won't browbeat you, torture you, or threaten you with jail time, but that doesn't mean the on-campus interview won't feel a bit like an interrogation. The room is usually cramped and spartan. Every word echoes, every movement is accentuated. It's enough to make a candidate forget about a job and start thinking about an alibi.

In such an environment, an interviewee's body language—how you cross your legs or sit in the chair—can actually make more of an impression on the interviewer than whatever well-rehearsed words might spill from your lips. Reams of psychological research suggest that while most facial expressions, body postures, and movements don't communicate information per se, they *do* advertise an attitude. And the wrong attitude can mean the difference between a fat signing bonus and a trip back to school—for a law degree.

A Hands-On Attitude. The most vexing question that many interviewees ask themselves isn't "Should I hold out for a company Lexus?" but rather "What should I do with my

by David Blend

hands?" Does folding them on the lap seem controlled, or passive? Does gesticulating make someone look energetic, or like an irate cabdriver? The answer depends on the interviewer, according to psychologist Laurence Stybel, president of Stybel, Peabody and Lincolnshire, a Boston-based career-management service that prepares senior executives for job interviews. Before deciding what to do with your hands, Stybel suggests that you analyze the language the company uses in its job description. If it tosses around energetic adjectives like *fast* and *rapid*, then sawing the air with your hands sends the right message because it indicates a willingness to be aggressive. If the company prefers *consistency* and *reliability*, place your hands quietly on your lap.

Lip Service.   Touching your lips can be an indicator of deception, says Mike Caro, known throughout the high-stakes gambling world as the Mad Genius of Poker. "If a speaker touches or obscures her face, especially her lips, there's a better-than-usual chance that you have just heard something that was uncomfortable to say, and that the speaker may have been lying or exaggerating," explains Caro. And he should know: He makes a living reading the subtle cues of his opponents. Two tips for appearing on the level: Show the palms of your hands during an interview, or touch your chest with your palm.

Armed and Dangerous.   Like the word "aloha," folding one's arms can communicate many things. Sadly, defensiveness, insecurity, inflexibility, and closed-mindedness aren't going to earn anybody a company trip to the Big Island. "It's almost like you're saying, 'What more do you people want from me?'" says Jody Swartzwelder, assistant director of campus recruiting for Arthur Andersen in Dallas.

The Handshake.   A recruiter's first impression of you is often formed when you shake hands—which is why you should never, ever extend a hand that is even slightly moist. Sweaty palms say one of three things: "I'm out of shape and frightened," "I am vaguely reptilian and therefore wholly untrustworthy," or "I am perhaps just a little bit too happy to meet you."

Angling for Position. Tipping back in the chair is a sure indicator of an interviewee's overconfidence and projects a subtle air of disdain. It's far better, recruiters say, to seem eager than arrogant. But leaning too far forward makes job candidates look as if they might pounce on their interviewers at any moment and demand to know "where the money's hidden." "You want to choose a moderate position that isn't too cocky but definitely lets the interviewer know that you are awake and aware," says Lauren Shapiro, who, as regional campus manager for Connecticut-based Deloitte Consulting, has supervised more than a thousand interviews.

Legwork. Which makes a stronger statement: legs crossed or feet planted on the floor? "It's hard to get comfortable in an interview, so choose whichever position puts you at ease," says Deloitte's Shapiro. She does caution, however, that if you cross your legs, they should be crossed all the way. "Resting your ankle on your knee conveys an overly casual attitude," she says. The most important thing, though, is to find a position and stick with it. Constant shifting can make an interviewee look, well, shifty.

Don't Touch Your Nose. Studies conducted at Chicago's Smell and Taste Treatment and Research Foundation show that touching the outside of the nose can be a prime indicator of lying. Guilt associated with deceptiveness triggers a rise in blood pressure, which then causes tissues in the nose to stretch and release histamine. The histamine causes itching, which in turn induces scratching. Recruiters may or may not be up on this research, but why find out the hard way?

Nice Gesture.   Job candidates should definitely convey enthusiasm for the position they're after. According to Andersen's Swartzwelder, pressing your fingers together to form a steeple not only shows interest but also suggests assertiveness and determination. Steepling can be overdone, however, especially when accompanied by a malevolent grin and the words "Your petty enterprise is no match for my cruel ambitions."

FIVE THINGS *NOT* TO DO IN AN INTERVIEW

1. When an interviewer gives you a cup of coffee, pour a little onto the floor and say, "For my homeys."
2. Integrate faux French phrases into your dialogue, such as, "I would say working hard is my *être de flume*."
3. Carry your resumé and personal belongings in a handkerchief wrapped around a stick. Lament the fact that riding the rails "ain't like it used to be."
4. Tell them that you're considering a day job but your real passion is your tortoise.
5. Solicit high fives. If the interviewer does not comply, sneer, "Lame."

---

by Justin Heimberg

Eye Contact.   Make it. Avoiding eye contact is unnerving for the interviewer and creates the impression that you're hiding something.

Show You Care.   If you get past the interview stage, you may have the pleasure of receiving a salary offer. Most candidates are savvy enough not to break into a rendition of "We Are the Champions" at this point. "The natural tendency would be to look away and act indifferent if an offer is more than a person expected," explains Caro. It's the equivalent, he says, of a poker player with a strong hand acting nonchalant when he wants an opponent to bet. If you want to up your own ante, it might be better to take a direct approach. After all, you're up against a pro.

DISASTER RELIEF: SURVIVAL STRATEGIES FOR RECRUITING CALAMITIES

You can prep all you want, but one screwup and you're soaked. What to do if you're late for an interview. Stumped by a question. Drenched by spilled coffee.

The outfit's perfect. The cover letter rocks. The pitch is smooth and witty and well rehearsed. If everything goes like it did in the mock interview, that job offer is in the bag. And yet, a bad break—traffic, head cold, sadistically difficult questions—can derail the best-laid plans and turn even a flawless candidate into an also-ran. Unless, of course, said candidate can turn disaster into opportunity. Twelve knotty problems and their slick solutions.

1. The interviewer poses a specific question. You have no idea what the answer is.

Some candidates stare at the ceiling and say, "I have to be honest. I have no idea." Others drift farther up the creek by trying to pull off a poker-faced bluff. You should do neither. If you can't demonstrate your knowledge, says Jeff Bloch, a consultant who trains big-name executives to handle the media, then dazzle the interviewers with your intelligence. If you're

by Russell Wild

asked, for instance, "What's the essence of the Modigliani-Miller valuation model?" an appropriate response might be: "I don't know enough about that particular model to discuss it in detail, but I can walk you through another valuation method that I think is extremely effective." Then explain why that method is close to your heart. "So many people get into trouble by filling the silence after a question with something that's wrong or that digs them deeper into a hole," explains Bloch. "No one expects you to be an encyclopedia. They do expect you to think on your feet, acknowledge mistakes, and perform under pressure."

2. The recruiter concludes the interview by saying, "You're staying at the Marquis Hotel, right? They've got a great bar. Fantastic margaritas. How about we finish our discussion there this evening?"

If you call the recruiter on this unethical, offensive behavior, you might win the moral high ground but lose the job. On the other hand, appearing to appreciate the flirtation—which some people wind up doing out of uneasiness rather than actual interest—might help you land the position but will lead to bad voodoo if you wind up getting the job. The best strategy is to dodge the advance while letting everyone save face. Judith Ré, an etiquette expert and the author of *Social Savvy*, suggests using body language as the first line of defense. Give off a firm, controlled air, she advises: "Turn to the interviewer, maintain direct eye contact, and keep your arms on the chair." (Resting them by your sides signals that you're open to the conversation, she says, while crossed arms are a sign of nervous defensiveness.) "Then say, 'I do have more questions, but I'm sure we can cover everything now.' This gets the message across but also clears a path for both of you to move on." You get the result you want without creating ill will. You can save that for later.

3. Thirty minutes into the interview, the recruiter calls you by the wrong name.

"All right, Elizabeth, so tell me what you think the biggest external threat to the company is," says the VP of sales. The trouble is, your name's Leslie. "An immediate correction is the best course of action," says Rebecca Butler, an MBA recruiter at UBS Warburg. Politely say, "It's Leslie," and move on. If it happens again? "You have to set the record straight immediately. Otherwise, the recruiter may not connect your interview with your name. It's about not getting lost in the shuffle." Butler suggests this clever response: "I know you see a lot of people, so I'd like to make sure you have the correct resumé in front of you. Leslie McIntosh, Michigan State, right?"

4. Your cell phone rings.

"Grab it and turn it off immediately," says Frank Luntz, a communications consultant and news analyst for MSNBC. Apologize and tuck it away. "Do not look to see who called. Make it clear that nothing could be more important than the interview," says Luntz. Next time: Turn it off beforehand.

5. You arrive late to the interview.

There's really no such thing as a "good" excuse—not traffic, not a broken alarm clock, not Ebola. And besides, banking on one misses the point. Everyone makes mistakes, and you can use the opportunity to show how you'd handle adversity as an employee. In short: Notify, own up, and move on. "Call as soon as you know you're going to be late, even if it's only by five minutes," says Dick McCracken, director of graduate career services for Indiana University's Kelley School. Briefly explain your situation, apologize, and then offer to reschedule. Say something like: "I realize I've thrown off your day, and I'm

happy to return at a more convenient time." You've acknowl-
edged your responsibility (as opposed to passing the buck) and
demonstrated that you're willing to be flexible. Be contrite but
not dramatic ("I'm sorry" is good; "I'm so, so sorry. I can't believe I did this, this never happens to me" is bad). And don't
give up hope. Says UBS Warburg's Butler: "Recruiters have
seen a lot. If you make the effort, we may let it pass."

6. An incredibly boring partner corners you at a recruiting party.

It's the big meet-and-greet, the single best opportunity to
shake many hands and make a lot of impressions. But as you try
to work the room, you're trapped by a retired partner who's
droning on about his cousin's bus trip to Spokane. The situation can be quickly resolved using the same tricks you probably relied on in high school, but with a bit more polish. First,
try a little misdirection, says veteran acting coach David Nack-
man. "Wave hello to a colleague on the other side of the
room," he says. Then return to your conversation. Wait a
minute or so, then explain that you absolutely must catch your
friend before he leaves. A more-sophisticated evacuation plan
requires deftly changing the subject, which provides a subtle
sense of closure and a natural breaking point. Then, start talking about a project the firm is working on and ask the person
which of his colleagues knows the most about it. "Thank the
person for his time and ask him to introduce you to his colleague," says Laurie Boockvar, associate director of MBA career services at Columbia Business School. It's a dignified
escape, and you depart showing a keen interest in the company.

7. The interviewer says something you know is incorrect.

"Our profits are greater than those of our three competitors
combined," intones the senior associate. But you, diligent in-

terviewee that you are, have done your homework: You know that he's referring to the company's market share, not its profits. Should you correct the person who holds your future in his hands? Damn straight. "For one thing, the interviewer might be testing you," says Jim Cameron, a former NBC news anchor who now coaches Fortune 500 executives on media relations. "If it's a factual error that you can contradict with solid data, then do it—confidently and politely." Begin your correction with "and" rather than "but"—as in "and so is your market share." The secret is to be right without showing the interviewer to be wrong. If after you've made the correction, the interviewer launches into an argument, drop it. "You don't want to come off as being rude," says Charley Buck, president of Charles Buck & Associates, a New York search firm. Battling the future boss will not win you points.

8. You make a gaffe. Something that is truly stupid.

When asked to name his favorite Disney character during a group interview with, yes, Disney, one MBA candidate offered, "Daffy Duck." "That's great," responded the Disney executive leading the discussion. "Warner Bros. is across the street." The student mumbled his apology while his fellow candidates snickered. Telling the Merrill Lynch recruiter during a final interview that you've always wanted to work at Goldman presents an equally thorny problem. The best course of action in this situation: Correct yourself quickly and make clear your commitment to Disney or Merrill or anybody by sprinkling details about the firm into the conversation. "The best move is to draw no further attention to your slip," says Seth Feit, an AOL talent scout. "It's the vision of the candidate trying to get himself out of the situation that the recruiter's going to remember." One more thing: Do not opt for the knee-jerk reaction and say you have an interview at Goldman tomorrow—even if you do. One candidate mentioned the wrong company name to American Management Association human resources director Manny Avramidis. "Then he compounded the problem by telling me about another interview he had with a competitor," says Avramidis. "I couldn't believe it."

9. You write a witty thank-you letter to a recruiter, sign it, drop it into the mailbox—then realize you put it into the wrong envelope.

Now what? Call the recruiter's secretary and explain what you've done and ask her to toss it, advises Dorothea Johnson, of the Protocol School of Washington, which provides etiquette seminars for executives and diplomats. "Even if the assistant does mention it to her boss," says Johnson, "it's less embarrassing than not having pointed out your error at all." Then let her know that you've already put the correct letter in the mail. Here's the trick: You increase your chances of success if you can restrain yourself and not call immediately. Instead, wait a day or two—by then the letter's arrival will be imminent. You don't want to risk the assistant's forgetting something like this.

10. You sneeze during an interview. And there's no Kleenex in sight.

"Cover your nose with your left hand," says Dana May Casperson, author of *Power Etiquette: What You Don't Know Can Kill Your Career.* "If you cover it with your right hand, the interviewer won't want to shake your hand at the end of the meeting. And covering with both hands or sneezing into your sleeve is just plain rude." The smart job candidate knows that it's better to ask to be excused and go to the rest room for two minutes than to be uncomfortable and self-conscious for the duration of the interview.

11. You're asked an illegal question.

You and the interviewer are really hitting it off, swapping stories about your recent weddings. "So, are you guys planning to have kids?" he asks. In some cases it's innocent banter. In others, the recruiter might be trying to gauge whether you'll be willing to put in eighty-hour weeks or whether the company might lose you to the demands of an infant. Either way, a recruiter can't legally ask about your race, your age, your religion, any disabilities you may have, or your plans to have children. But, in this case, should you point that out? Not directly, says Sally Haver, a vice president at the Ayers Group, a New York recruiting firm. She recommends speaking to the interviewer's intent with a response like: "My record makes clear that my personal obligations have never interfered with my work. One of my strengths is my ability to separate my professional and personal lives." By addressing the interviewer's concerns, explains Haver, "you make it clear that you understand his question and that it's inappropriate to ask." That said, if you feel a recruiter has asked an illegal or offensive question, you're well within your rights to end the interview right then and there.

12. You spill coffee on your lap.

Turning to greet the managing director as she enters the conference room, you knock your coffee onto your new Armani suit. Saying, "Well, so much for a good first impression. Did I get the job?" is a smart way of putting people at ease. Don't wait for someone else to take care of the problem: Quickly ask where they keep the paper towels. This response shows self-sufficiency and a sense of responsibility, says Mary Tenopyr, former director of employee-candidate testing for AT&T. If an associate runs off to get towels, you should go, too—you don't want to be sitting around in a mess you created, waiting for someone else to take action. "Continuing the conversation where it left off," Tenopyr says, "makes clear that the interview is more important to you than the coffee spill." Do not, under any circumstances, remove your pants.

INTERVIEWS GONE BAD

Mismatched socks? You should be so lucky . . .

Tongue-Tied.   Wade Crosson straightened his tie as he waited for interviewer Laura Guerin to ask another question. Usually a nontraditional dresser, Crosson had selected fairly conservative business attire for his meeting with the web-consulting firm Razorfish. Yet as he discussed his qualifications for the human resources position, Crosson noticed that the steel stud in his tongue had detached. He arched his tongue forward in an attempt to retrieve it, only to feel the jewelry roll back toward his throat. Whereupon he promptly started to choke. By the time Guerin returned with a glass of water, Crosson had swallowed the jewelry whole. He came clean and, having demonstrated a fair amount of composure, earned himself a position at the firm.

Muchas Problemas.   For fifteen minutes, Anand David, then a recruiter for the energy-trading firm Enron, grilled the prospective hire about debt ratios, capital markets, and corporate valuation. The candidate's concise responses were as impressive as his resumé, which boasted, among other things, a proficiency in German and French. Then David's colleague posed a question in German. "Uh, oh, well, I haven't really practiced my German in a while," the MBA mumbled. *"Pas de problème,"* David replied. The student, stunned, stared incomprehensibly, and the room fell silent. "Okay," said David, "that clears up all of our questions."

by David Blend and Alexis Offen

Royal Flush. Halfway through a final-round interview at a top New York investment bank, Marshall was told by his interviewer, a vice president, that "something had come up" and they would have to continue the session elsewhere. Marshall duly followed the person around the corner, through the hallway, to . . . the men's room. Taking it in stride, Marshall stood outside the stall and continued to answer questions and sell himself with conviction. He got the offer.

Silent Treatment. Things were going great during his final round at a major bank, when Sean was shown into the office of a managing director, who proceeded to tell him . . . precisely nothing. Not a word. Sean asked if he was in the right place. Icy stare. Resisting the urge to panic, Sean took a deep breath and began: "Well, if you are going to evaluate me for this position, there are some things I think you should know about me. I'm a finance major, am vice president of my school's student body, and looking for a position in sales at a top bank. I think I would be a valuable hire because . . ." After twenty-five minutes, a coordinator came to get him and took him to the next (and last) interview of the day. Sean got the job.

Tossing Cookies. As the interview was about to begin, the candidate excused himself to go to the men's room. Five minutes later he returned, but with a slightly, um, different look. The candidate was pale and shaken—and on the right shoulder of his navy sports coat was a small fleck of vomit. "Are you okay?" asked one of the recruiters for BDM, a technical consulting firm in McLean, Virginia. "Yes, yes, fine," said the prospective hire, whose breath left a more memorable impression than his performance.

JOB HUNTERS FROM HELL

Face-to-face with a recruiter's worst nightmare . . .

Looking for Love. Five minutes into her interview with a first-year MBA, Danielle Domingue knew he wasn't right for the job. The candidate, too, realized he hadn't prepared adequately for Deloitte Consulting's rigorous screening process. "This interview isn't going well," the student conceded, "so I might as well score points in other areas." Domingue, no longer a recruiter with Deloitte, peered up from her notes. "You're definitely one of the best-looking recruiters on campus," the student said, looking Domingue in the eye. "Wanna go out for a drink tonight?"

Mommie Dearest. A few years back, Lauren White, then a recruiter for Barclays Global Investors, mailed out a handful of rejection letters, including one to a student at the University of California—Davis. Two weeks later, White picked up the phone and got a steaming earful from an irate woman. White realized that the caller was not a disappointed job seeker but the mother of the rejected UC—Davis student. Mommy demanded to know why her daughter hadn't been selected for the position. "We keep our hiring decisions confidential," White responded, diplomatically ending the conversation. The woman called back every day for the next two weeks.

Fat Chance. The moment the hiring manager for Nortel Networks offered the candidate a strategic-analyst position, the tension in the room eased. Suddenly relaxed, the new hire, a thirty-something man of medium build, opened up to his soon-to-be colleague and described in painstaking detail the

by David Blend and Alexis Offen

exercise program he had used to shed weight. "Matter of fact," he said, "you should look into the program yourself." The heavyset recruiter tried to change the subject, but the candidate went on and on about "exercise" and "fat." To end the discussion, the recruiter said, "We'll be in touch about the contract." When the man wouldn't stop talking about weight loss, the recruiter retracted the offer.

10

Advanced Recruiting Tactics

....

TWENTY-EIGHT TIPS
FOR GETTING THE JOB YOU WANT

Ever imagine listening to a team of all-star recruiters, MBAs, senior managers, and professors talk about winning job-search strategies? Pull up a chair:

From start to finish, the recruiting process is loaded with established guidelines, deadlines, schedules, and rules. But beyond the advice doled out by career counselors and those stale how-to books, there's a vast pool of unwritten knowledge handed down with a wink by benevolent graduates and recruiters alike. These nuggets are off the record and between the lines—and could mean the difference between coming in for a second interview and coming in second place. But to get the goods, you have to know the right people. We do. In fact, many of our recruiting experts have such high positions that they wouldn't let their names be used. You'll soon see why.

Laying the Groundwork

1. Need to call a recruiter? Do it before nine or after five. That way, you won't get her assistant. (Assistants almost never make hiring decisions.) If no one answers, just leave a mes-

---

by David Blend, *MBA Jungle*

sage. Don't hang up and call back five more times. Ever hear of caller ID?

2. Make friends with a second-year who's already received offers from companies you want to work for. Why? Because many recruiters ask new hires who the stars of the incoming class are, and you want yours to be the name they drop. Don't disguise your motives. "It's perfectly within protocol for a first-year to ask a second-year to have a beer or a cup of coffee to talk about a company," says one NYU Stern '99 grad. "If I like you, I'll definitely pass your name along, but don't e-mail me your resumé out of the clear blue and expect me to submit it to the company."

3. Calling distant relatives or friends of friends of friends to network is a good move, but don't spend more than two sentences explaining your connection to the person. "Within thirty seconds, I should know that you're good for the job because you're at the top of your class, not because you used to play on my kid's soccer team," says a campus recruiter for a major bank.

4. Companies that recruit on-campus adhere to rigid schedules—but that's no reason you should. "A month before they hit campus, write a letter or make a call to each company's rep to introduce yourself," says Antoinette Chambers, director of MBA career services at the University of Tennessee. "They'll be impressed with your interest and initiative, and when the recruiters show up, I guarantee they'll remember your name."

5. From José Andino, the human resources manager at CNBC.com, who sees ten to fifteen recruits a week:

"People spend more time investigating the type of house they're going to buy than the company that's hopefully going to help them buy it. And the ones who do conduct research usually confine it to the Internet. These days, that's not enough. You'd be surprised how much information you can get from calling a receptionist or chatting with a security guard—they often know more than you might expect about the company culture, and they're usually willing to talk. The first question to ask: Do people at this company generally seem happy? You'll get a lot of mileage out of that one."

6. At most companies, you're pitching yourself to two audiences: human resources and the hiring manager. So prepare two resumés, advises Deanne Rosenberg, president of Deanne Rosenberg, Inc., in Wareham, Massachusetts. One should list your credentials and experience; the other should emphasize your ability to learn. HR is simply trying to fill an order: two MBAs with x, y, and q experience, Rosenberg says. In a single glance at your resumé, they should see that you have x, y, and q, so go ahead and detail your course selection within your marketing major. Get more creative with the resumé for the hiring manager. Show how you used your marketing knowledge to create a new branding concept for the last company you worked for. The hiring manager is interested in how prospective employees think and how they've taken initiative.

7. At every possible opportunity, quantify your accomplishments. This makes what you're saying instantly credible and tangible. Saying "Acquired ten new accounts for my brokerage last year, which ranked me first in the group" is much better than "Led group in account acquisitions." Why? Recruiters are constantly comparing candidates with one another, and they'll subconsciously associate your name with the phrase "first in the group."

The Cattle Calls

8. If you know you want to work for a specific firm, go to the company's presentation, no matter how much you already know about the firm. When an interviewer asks if you were there—and they will ask—your "Yes" will be an honest answer. Says a former associate at one of the biggest banks on the Street: "I only missed one, and sure enough, I was asked about it in the interview. It was definitely a smudge on my record."

9. Four words about business cards: Never offer, always carry. And while we're on the subject, buy a simple business-card holder—silver, gold, or leather, monogram-free.

10. Following a corporate presentation, don't approach the big-deal partner to chat him/her up and get her card; thirty other people will be doing precisely that. Instead, peg one of his/her subordinates, who likely has a hand in the early stages of the process. "You'll get quality time with a person who counts right now rather than a quick handshake from a big shot you won't be dealing with until later," says a former recruiting-team leader for a major strategy consulting company.

11. At large recruiting events, swallow your sartorial pride and wear the damn name tag. If they aren't preprinted and you have to make your own, write your last name twice as large as your first. Then stick the thing over your right breast. That way, when you reach out your hand to shake, your name will jump directly into the person's line of sight.

12. RECRUITER: What would you like to drink?
You: Um, what kind of beer is there? No wait, maybe I'll have a gin and, well, actually . . .

Wrong, wrong, wrong. When it comes to alcohol consumption, know what you want to order. It doesn't matter if it's a scotch or a spritzer, make it sound like you've asked for it a thousand times before. Then don't ask for it more than twice again that night.

13. If you can, mention a recent book or article that the hiring manager probably hasn't read. Pique his interest in it. This creates a natural follow-up opportunity, namely, you sending the article to the hiring manager the next day along with a (very) short note.

The Interview

14. The rule of thumb for addressing prospective employers: "For someone no more than two levels above the position you want, use his or her first name," says one Silicon Alley start-

up CEO. "For someone three levels or more up, use 'Mr.' or 'Ms.' until they instruct you otherwise." Never use "Homeslice" or "Sweetie."

15. If you don't immediately know the answer to a question during a case interview, look down while you think of something to say. The natural tendency is to look up, but politicians and other seasoned public speakers are coached to stare at the floor. It gives the appearance of being deep in thought.

16. From an adjunct professor of marketing at a top-twenty B-school: "In a second interview, ask the recruiter why you were selected. This, of course, takes some finesse. Don't ask in a 'Why me? I'm not worthy' sort of way. Just be curious and confident. This will get your inquisitor talking about you—and let you know exactly what you should be talking to her about."

17. Acceptable reasons for not being available on the first date the recruiter proposes for a second interview:

Wedding (yours only)
Death (yours only)

18. Whether it's asked during a "friendly" recruiting dinner or in a Super Saturday grilling, the hobby question is always a trick. Don't talk about the last novel you read or your praying mantis collection. These are solo activities. "Companies want team players," explains the president of a small high-tech recruiting firm. "Talk about something that demonstrates your ability to work with others." Even if skiing's your sport, turn it into group activity by mentioning how you organized nine friends to go in on a condo last winter and hit the slopes en masse.

19. From Danielle Martin, the human resources manager at BTS USA, a management-consulting company in Stamford, Connecticut: "In the final stage of our recruiting process, each candidate gives a brief presentation on a company of her choice in front of five consultants in our firm. One candidate, who had just been introduced to the group for the first time,

addressed each person by name when answering questions. To me that showed she paid attention to detail, and that she could keep her composure when interrupted by questions—both skills we look for." This goes for the entire recruiting process, of course. When someone asks who else you've met at the company (you can count on this), use the clever mnemonic devices you've created, and rattle off seventeen names as if reciting your home phone number.

Interview Aftermath

20. "Save your best question for right after an interview, when, say, you're being walked to the elevator," says Amy Giering, an NYU Stern '01 grad. "The interviewer will be more focused on your question, because she's not thinking about the ten things she has to ask you." It'll also show the interviewer that you're uncommonly inquisitive and that you think well on your feet. Plus, it makes an excellent final impression.

21. Never call a recruiter from a cell phone. Ever. And, duh, don't leave it on when you are in the company of one.

22. "Dear Mr. _____: The purpose of this letter is to thank you for the opportunity to interv——." Whoa, Officious One, stop right there. Everyone writes cookie-cutter thank-you letters. More effective is the "influence letter," in which the candidate makes all the carefully articulated points that weren't made in the interview. In one page, restate your most relevant qualifications. Then advance the discussion you had by taking it one step further: "I was thinking about your question concerning the plant in Mexico, and I think one solution might be——."

23. Don't underestimate the power of a classy piece of stationery.

24. If you're waiting for callbacks from prospective employers, instruct your housemates to say politely that you're

(a) at the library, (b) out showing your business plan, (c) not back from Davos.

25. Instruct said housemates never to use the following words or phrases:

A. Probation officer
B. Tequiza
C. "Can"

26. True story from a '95 Southern Methodist University B-school grad:

"I was dead-set on getting a job with Towers Perrin, but the company said it was only hiring Ivy Leaguers and students from other schools in the Northeast. So I flew to Chicago on spring break—with no appointment scheduled—and walked into the company's headquarters wearing my best suit. I told the receptionist in the vaguest of terms that I was in the building "on business" and wanted to see if I could talk to the managing director. I actually got through and met one of the partners. A few weeks later, I got the job."

Moral: Do whatever it takes.

27. True story from a Wharton '97 grad:

"I was at a career conference at Deloitte Consulting, and as I was leaving, I noticed the guy I had interviewed with a couple of days earlier standing out front. He was trying to hail a cab at five o'clock on a Friday, and obviously having no luck. I had driven to the event, so I sprinted five blocks to my car, pulled up in front of him, and offered him a lift. He was trying to catch a train, so he jumped in. I chatted him up the whole ride. A week later I got an offer."

Moral: Do whatever it takes.

28. Let's say you're at the racetrack and you've got $72.50 riding on horse number four, a five-to-one shot who's neck-and-neck with another horse. So you're rooting for the four horse. Good. Now imagine you've got $100,000 on that horse. Suddenly you're rooting for your pony to win with

every fiber of your being. Is that how much you want this job? That's what a prospective employer should think.

DINING FOR DOLLARS

The recruiting dinner is just one more tricky step in the many-staged interview process. The stakes are high, time is tight, the competition is merciless, and one faux pas can cost you the job. Your hostess will seat you now.

Play your cards right and you will be spending plenty of time in nice restaurants, eating great food on the company's dime. For many top firms, presentations, question and answer sessions, and informal interviewing are done primarily within a few feet of a place setting. Play your cards right at these meals, and you will be spending plenty of time deciding which offers to accept. Then you can spend plenty more time in nice restaurants—this time on the other side of the table.

How important are these dinners? How about extremely. "We all know that the resumé is not perfect information," says Caitlin McLaughlin, vice president and manager for MBA recruiting at Salomon Smith Barney. "The dinner is almost reverse recruiting." That is, recruiters already know what their guests look like on paper, so the real test is seeing how well they handle themselves in a social situation.

OK, so the dinners are important. How hard can it be to nail them? The savvy student shows up, pushes around some pasta, waxes eloquent about the Nasdaq, and hits 'em with the charm train so hard their heads hurt. Right?

McLaughlin has attended hundreds of dinners, and although many candidates handle themselves with aplomb, she has also seen the ugly side of the recruiting dinner: the student bright enough to be invited to an open-bar reception but demented enough to order the $185 cognac; the guy who was

by Paul Scott

caught trying to change place cards so he'd be seated closer to the company big shot; not to mention countless other missteps, blunders, and screwups.

Besides, if recruiting dinners were such a cakewalk, the firms wouldn't bother with them. All things being equal— grades, resumés, and test scores—how you handle yourself between the bar and the coat check can determine whether you receive a job offer. With so much at stake and with so many potential pitfalls, it takes a deft combination of tact, assertiveness, and savoir faire to shine in these circumstances. In other words, eat before leaving home, because it's not about the food.

> **INSIDER TIP.** As with other parts of the recruiting process, the mindset of those judging you is: How will this person act in front of clients? Think of it as playacting. You are an associate at their firm, they are a client.

Something to Chew On

"The typical recruit going through the process could easily have ten meals with us," says Dana Ellis, director of recruiting for Arthur Andersen, which hires 300 MBAs straight out of school every year. "It's a great forum for exchanging information on many levels." One of those levels is etiquette. Considering that a candidate will likely be wining and dining clients, manners are something a recruiter can't help but notice.

Everyone knows not to chew with an open mouth, but consider a few less obvious deal breakers that recruiters have noted: mopping up sauce with the bread; cutting an entrée into a lot of bites rather than one bite at a time; eating too quickly. Regardless of what looks enticing on the menu, avoid ordering soup, spaghetti, lobster, ribs—anything that could possibly make you look like a slob. And while recruiters profess not to judge people by their menu choices—for instance, deciding that someone is a girlie-man because he ordered the salad as an entrée—they do notice the matter of price. "Anything in the extreme draws attention," says Ellis. "If everyone's having the $9 cheeseburger and some guy orders a $35 steak with an $18 appetizer, it looks bad."

On the subject of looking bad, eat what is served, however undercooked, charred, or otherwise unpalatable. "On the whole, fussy is bad," adds Ellis. "If someone's picky about their food, maybe they'll be picky about their job assignments, or who they'll work with, or about having to make a 7 A.M. meeting." If you're a vegetarian and the recruiting dinner is in a steak house? "Well, my heart goes out to you," says Ellis. "But I wouldn't make a big deal about it."

If a waiter happens to serve you the wrong item altogether, or something that's flat-out inedible, bring it to his attention—but do so subtly. Although some candidates evidently think it makes them look like a take-charge type, don't rigorously hail the server; eye contact and a discreet tilt of the head will carry the day. (Rumors exist of firms arranging for this to happen to see how a candidate handles mix-ups.) "Err on the side of being too polite to the servers. Even the mildest condescension toward a waiter is a huge negative," says McLaughlin. "One of the things we're looking for is the capacity to deal with people at all levels. When somebody takes a superior attitude, you have to wonder how well they're going to work in a team at our company."

Concomitant with this are a few little things, like remembering to tip the coat-check person, if you are at an establishment where this is common. Just remembering to say "Thank you for dinner" can make a positive impression. "Having been to hundreds of fancy dinners, it's easy to feel jaded," says one recruiter at a top management-consulting firm, "when someone acknowledges the effort we make it doesn't go unnoticed."

Drink, but Don't Be Merry

"A lot of companies will let you have a few drinks to see how you do," says Charles Sacarello of Charles & Associates, a New York–based image-consulting firm that whips boorish spouses of CEOs into shape. "They look for whether you loosen your tie or take off your jacket when no one else has. That sort of thing."

When it comes to alcohol, most recruiters advise following the host's lead before ordering—that is, having a beer or cocktail only if the rep does so first—though abstaining is not necessarily a negative mark. A few other points to remember: Cup your hand when squeezing a lime wedge over a gin and tonic. Drink beer from a glass. When it's time to head to the dinner table, leave cocktails on the bar. Once seated, drink what the host drinks with the meal. (This is not the time to showcase one's individuality, let alone one's knowledge of rare Lebanese wines.) Refrain from completely draining the wineglass at any point during the meal. Refrain from refilling your own glass (let the waiter do that). And by all means, do refrain from that human-garbage-pail, bottoms-up move when it's time to go.

A Little Practice

It's an odd contradiction: While the American workforce is becoming better educated, better traveled, and increasingly professional, knowledge of basic manners doesn't seem to have kept pace.

"I've had a client tell me, 'This person is brilliant and handsome, but we took him to a restaurant and everything changed. His tie was over his shoulder, his face was over his dinner plate, he ordered wine when he shouldn't have,'" says Sue Fox, author of *Business Etiquette for Dummies* and president of Etiquette Survival, a California-based company that helps Silicon Valley executives polish their acts. "This was a guy who was going to be called upon to host the company's Japanese clients—and they would have been mortified."

Those with a tendency to get spots on their ties or who feel even slightly uncomfortable dining in business attire might consider practicing. One way is to eat at home in a jacket for a week. The producers of the original James Bond films are said to have made Sean Connery do as much, and it clearly paid off for him. It's worth rehearsing your manners, too. While recruiters downplay the formality of their outings as well as their own knowledge of the minutiae of etiquette, the professional manner-meisters claim that future employers look for polish without knowing it. "Companies are trying to find future executives, people who will project the image of the firm," says Sacarello. "Bone up on this stuff ahead of time," adds Fox. "Because you don't want to be distracted by thinking about what glass to use while you're being interviewed. You want to spend that time asking smart questions."

As it happens, recruiters say, they're more likely to schedule meals at noisy, hip places than at morguelike restaurants where a person can hear the silver clink. So candidates can look out of step if they show up dressed for a board meeting. Recruiters agree that if someone is uncertain about what to wear, it's entirely sensible to scout the restaurant beforehand or to call the person organizing the dinner to ask about appropriate dress.

Dining with Sharks

As if social blunders weren't enough to worry about, there are fellow classmates to deal with. Where the cautious student may find himself laboring not to appear either overzealous or underambitious, there's a decent chance that the competition is going to be overtalking, undermining, and out-hustling him for the job. B-school lore is rife with stories of job candidates acting to advance their interests at the expense of their class-mates: from the student who kept the date of a recruiting reception to herself to the guy who put up fake flyers announcing a change of venue for a dinner.

Perhaps most annoying are those who think nothing of striding into the middle of your three minutes with the recruiter and hijacking the conversation. Should this happen, do not roll your eyes. Do not throw an elbow. Do not get caught up in the petty race for airtime. Stay composed and polite, and remember that if the guy looks obnoxious to you, he'll look obnoxious to the recruiter.

That said, you don't want to squander your few minutes with a recruiter. "Don't go without having three points to make about yourself," says Ronna Lichtenberg, author of *Work Would Be Great If It Weren't for the People*, a lucid guide to office politics. "It might be something you are skilled at or would like to do in a work setting, or an aspect of the company you'd like to know more about. Whatever it is, if you have three positives in the cupboard, you'll feel more in control of the conversation."

And if the feeding frenzy starts to get out of hand? First, resist any urge to make fellow candidates look bad. It's a strategy beyond the skills of most, and one that can backfire badly. "You don't look good by attacking someone," says Lichtenberg. "If someone comes after you—say, someone tries to make something you said sound dumb—don't defend your comment. Instead, say something like, 'I guess you have a lot more experience with this topic than I do, why don't you tell me more?' Bullies and braggers don't have a sense of proportion. They'll roll on and on, and hang themselves." And if another student is hogging the floor? "Let them go on all they like as long as you've made your points," she says. "Don't worry about the other student. It's the recruiter who matters."

At most recruiting dinners, the company will send along a variety of representatives from different levels of the organization and rotate them from table to table during the predinner mingling. Avoid the mistake of snubbing the junior-level associate to chum up to the big dog. "Everybody within our firm is equally important—that means the staff setting up the dinner as well as the managing directors," says SSB's McLaughlin. "Don't race past a VP to start schmoozing an MD. We're all there together and everyone's opinion counts when we trade notes afterward." McLaughlin points out another risk inherent in racing up to the chief: "If you sit next to the senior partner but aren't comfortable talking about the highest levels of business, you have more of a chance of blowing it than if you sit next to a junior associate who's recently out of business school." Not to mention that it's far easier for him to picture you in his seat a year down the line.

B-SCHOOL ENTREPRENEURS:
SIX THINGS TO DO WHILE STILL IN SCHOOL

If you're serious about running your own business someday, you don't have to wait until you finish your MBA to get started. In fact, B-school is the perfect place to begin the process. After all, how many other times in your life will you be surrounded by a captive group of advisers *and* bright, talented leaders itching to get involved in the Next Big Thing?

Six things you can do to get the train out of the station:

1. Join the entrepreneurship club

Most business schools have a club for entrepreneurs that sets up informative and inspirational lectures by entrepreneurial alumni, sponsors tutorials on securing venture capital, and offers tips on writing a business plan. If you're trying to find partners to make the leap with you, fellow club members might be prime candidates—many probably share your spirit of adventure and willingness to take risks. You can also learn from classmates who have already started businesses. And getting involved in the leadership of the club can give you exposure to prominent investors and entrepreneurs.

2. Take entrepreneurship classes

It's often said that you can't teach someone to be an entrepreneur. True enough, it's unlikely that any professor can teach someone charisma and imbue an appetite for risk in a single semester. And these qualities won't even go very far if your business plan is a windy 200 pages. Before you blindly go forth into the world of valuations and VC rounds, it doesn't hurt to establish a thorough grounding in the basics. Whether you're expanding the family business or envisioning the wireless killer app, classes like "Entrepreneurial Management" and "Financing Your Venture" will help you master the fundamentals. In class, ask questions relevant to your idea, and arrange to meet with professors outside of class. These courses are often taught and visited by entrepreneurs who are eager to share their experiences and advise students on their ventures.

3. Use the resources of a small-business development center

Many schools have a dedicated small-business development center (SBDC) whose purpose is to assist entrepreneurs in the community. SBDC staff may evaluate proposals, edit business plans, and even act as presentation coaches—all free of charge. A great way to get firsthand experience is to work at the SBDC, perhaps as an intern between your first and second years or as a part-time consultant during the school year.

4. Attend entrepreneurial networking events

Knowing the right people can be the difference between a soaring success and an idea that never gets off the ground. Some schools hold weekly brown-bag lunches where entrepreneurs speak about how they built their businesses, how it's going— real-life case-study stuff. Stack the odds in your favor by meeting as many people as possible who might be helpful to you. You never know who you might meet at a local chamber of commerce breakfast or your school's annual entrepreneurship conference. Several entrepreneur-centered events make the job even easier with color-coded name tags: Anyone who's there to look for funding wears one color, while those who seek to invest in start-ups wear another. Don't even ask about the paisley tags.

5. Spread the word—on campus and to alumni

Stealth mode is good to a degree, but if no one knows about your idea, it's a sure bet that it won't get funded. Use discretion, but do spread the word. Tell your classmates about your idea and tap into your school's alumni network to find other potential sources of funding and staff. You can even use mbajungle.com's MBA Network tool to search for B-school alumni and current students at other schools—you might just scroll right to the perfect COO for your nascent company.

6. Enter business-plan competitions

Once you have a plan in hand, consider entering business-plan competitions. These come in many flavors, but your own school is a good place to start. Often sponsored and judged by top-flight incubators or VCs, these competitions are a good way to get prime exposure for your idea right from the start. Even if you don't make it to the final round, the pressure of a deadline is a good motivational tool to get your business plan finished and to hone your presentation skills. Plus, more and more schools now organize competitions with prize money and exposure to investors (Wharton, NYU–Stern, UCLA–Anderson, Cornell-Johnson, Columbia, Berkeley-Haas, MIT–Sloan, and Harvard are some examples), so although the setting may be academic, the stakes are anything but.

Then look past your school to other competitions, both local and national. Morgan Stanely Dean Witter, CIBC World Markets, Garage.com, and McKinsey & Co. all sponsor competitions, as does Jungle Interactive, whose last winner took home more than $25,000 in seed money and an offer of $250,000 in angel financing from a group of the judges.

11

Working Abroad

....

TAKING THE JOB HUNT OVERSEAS

Looking to land a spot abroad? There are many paths away from the home country. Here's a look at the options.

When she spied the security guards with sawed-off shotguns patrolling the grounds of her workplace, Laura Marshall (Wharton '00) realized just how different her MBA summer internship was from that of her classmates back at home. "I was consulting for a small construction company in Lima," she says. "I'd done research about working in Peru, but nothing could have prepared me for the reality of how business gets conducted there." Poverty, economic uncertainty, and corruption were part of the daily experience. "My time abroad gave an entirely new perspective on how things are done at companies in the U.S."

Some 15 percent of graduates from American business schools take their first jobs outside the United States. But whether it's a summer internship in South America or a full-time job in Japan, tracking down a position overseas can be an adventure in its own right. So here are the steps you should take if you're thinking about working outside the United States.

Understand the Options

There are many ways you can work globally. The most straightforward option is working for a big consulting firm, such as Accenture, PricewaterhouseCoopers, or McKinsey & Co., which all have offices around the world staffed with MBAs. (General rule of thumb: the less developed the country, the more opportunity for responsibility and personal advancement.) You can apply directly to the firm's country office or aim for a spot with the company in the United States and try to transfer to your nation of choice.

Other MBA industries—such as banking, marketing, and manufacturing—offer travel opportunities (but not with as much flexibility in consulting, where you can do one-project stints, a one-year stay, or an extended arrangement). But U.S. firms (such as Goldman Sachs and J. P. Morgan Chase) as well as European-headquartered companies (ING Barings, UBS Warburg) recruit for their offices around the globe. And firms such as General Electric, Alcoa, and Coca-Cola have been doing international-rotation programs for years. That is, they will send managers to company offices around the world for a few months or a few years in order to expand their knowledge of the business. Caution: Be sure to understand beforehand what your options will be *after* you finish the international rotation. Finally, you may choose to work for a local firm in a foreign land. This is the biggest wild card. It's risky and can require a lot of research and perseverance to get these jobs.

Use Your School Resources

Many schools' career centers have programs to assist students wishing to work abroad. At American University's Kogod School of Business, for example, the career office has an internship coordinator whose sole responsibility is helping students find opportunities in other countries. Your school's generalists can certainly provide some guidance. Of course, the alumni network is probably the best resource of all. The alums working in your target country went through the same process and will therefore have advice, contacts, and local knowledge. Also seek out the international and exchange students on your own campus.

Try a Foreign Exchange

Many B-schools have exchange programs with other schools. This is an excellent opportunity to try living in another country and to explore job opportunities at ground zero. One term in a structured learning environment will give you a good taste of what life would be like for an extended stay.

Go to B-School in the Target Country

Another approach is to take the full plunge and get your MBA in the country of choice. Several of the world's top business programs (e.g., INSEAD, London Business School) are outside the United States. In addition, many newly accredited programs are sprouting up around the world—mainly in or around the big business centers in Asia and Europe. A number of established U.S. B-schools are seeing a growth opportunity in catering to the global business crowd and have launched satellite programs in hot spots such as London, Paris, and Singapore. Attending an accredited program in Canada, Europe, or Asia will provide a solid education while allowing plenty of time to build contacts, visit companies, and soak up the culture.

Job Hunt on the Ground

"Fly to the city if possible, and set up meetings to make your case while you are there," says Sujata Bhatia, a recent Wharton grad who landed a full-time banking position in England. "This was the single biggest factor behind my ability to get the job in London." Being on location gives you several advantages over the remote hunt. First, many jobs aren't advertised abroad. Second, a personal visit indicates an applicant's commitment to working in the country. Besides, interviewing face-to-face with the employer is always preferred.

Get Your Story Straight

Because of the additional expense involved in hiring foreigners, companies want to know your level of commitment. If they think an applicant is simply after a one-year experience abroad, they'll be less inclined to put you on their payroll. Be able to make a convincing argument about your desire to stay with the company.

Learn the Language

Not speaking the language doesn't necessarily blackball you, but it's unlikely to help your cause. Taking classes shows recruiters that you are at least making an effort. By all means do so. Fortunately, once you have the job, many companies will help pay for further instruction with a tutor.

Plan Ahead

Count on all the normal aspects of a job hunt taking twice as long as they do at home. Give yourself strict deadlines, leaving extra time for country research at the beginning and paperwork at the end. And once you have an offer, you'll have a whole host of new issues to deal with, such as securing visas and permits and finding housing.

Get Visas and Permits. Labor laws vary greatly from country to country. Employers will help with the appropriate working papers if they make an offer. But many small companies don't have the resources to facilitate this. The best source of information on visas and working papers is the country's embassy in your home country. Check their web sites. Many countries also have economic development or trade organizations whose mission is to facilitate country-to-country business exchange. Utilize their resources. However, in some cases, employing foreigners is not an option, so you may need to get creative, for example, by working as a consultant. As a last resort, some MBAs told us, they arrange to be paid under the table.

BEFORE YOU HIT THE ROAD, HIT THE WEB

Sites with general background information on working abroad and helpful links:

University of California–Irvine's International Opportunities
   Program page: *http://www.cie.uci.edu/iop/work.html*
The Riley Guide:
   http://www.dbm.com/jobguide/intlinfo.html
U.S. State Department:
   http://www.state.gov/employment.cfm

Sites with job postings:
Iagora: *http://www.iagora.com/index.html::lang=en*
EMDS: *http://www.emdsnet.com*
OverseasJobs.com:
   http://www.overseasjobs.com/do/where
Centers for Disease Control and Prevention:
   www.cdc.gov/travel/

For information on these organizations and the location of
   foreign embassies in the U.S., go to:
   http://www.chamberofcommerce.com

If you don't have your passport yet, you'll want to get that ball rolling as soon as possible. www.travel.state.gov/passport_services.html and www. passportexpress.com are two sites that can help.

Also, check out the career sites of international business schools. Even if they don't let you access their job postings, they may give you ideas about which companies recruit MBAs in that market.

Line Up Housing.   If you are offered a position abroad, be prepared to go there early to secure housing—and, in some cases, a housing permit. A good time to get the lay of the land is during the interview. Ask if the company offers housing or relocation assistance and speak with employees about finding a place to stay.

Get a Clean Bill of Health.   When planning to work abroad, particularly in developing nations, get all the appropriate immunizations and medications. "We recommend that students check our web site for information on immunizations and also for news about disease outbreaks around the globe," says a spokesperson for the Centers for Disease Control and Prevention in Atlanta, Georgia. It's also a good idea to leave copies of your health records and other identification documents with friends or family before you leave.

THE LONG WAY HOME

For the 75,000 international students at American business schools, leaving family and culture behind is agonizing. But going back may be even tougher.

In the upside-down world that awaits the international student who takes an American diploma and heads home, the jobs come with big titles and small markets. The banks give free rein but often have no cash. Deals need to be closed quickly, but local custom dictates arriving at meetings three hours late. All those international-economics classes were fine, but the professors forgot to explain a few things: like how in the hell you're supposed get the job done with spotty phone service; crapshoot e-mail; an on-again, off-again power supply; a roller-coaster currency; and regulators who never saw a bribe they didn't like.

So, why go back—especially when many fellow classmates from overseas will be jockeying to stay in the United States,

by Paul Scott

and companies seeking international perspectives—or just diversity—will be showing them all kinds of love?

As Billy Vaisberg, a Venezuelan with an MBA from the University of Michigan and CEO of the Caracas-based ForeignMBA.com, puts it, "The opportunities for MBAs in less-developed countries are extremely attractive."

The compensation often starts with those perks that fall closest to the heart—family, friends, and familiar food. Maybe the chance to do the homeland some good. Maybe the itch for adventure—less Indiana State, more Indiana Jones. Maybe the bet that a U.S. degree means an elevator ride to the top of something small but powerful.

So what's it like to head home with a shiny diploma and a head full of big ideas? Below, the stories of four MBAs who made the move and how they're faring half a world away from where they earned their degrees.

Carlos Caballero, University of Michigan '97, Lima, Peru

Things looked remarkably different back in May 1997, when Carlos Caballero received his MBA. "Returning to Peru seemed like a great decision," he says. "The business community was experiencing a revitalization within the top levels of management, and middle management needed prodding into the ways of the global economy." In other words, Peru would welcome an American-trained MBA with open arms and brimming pocketbooks.

In the three years since, Caballero's career has undergone a meteoric rise, the likes of which his former classmates back in the United States can only dream about. He reached his aggressive five-year goal of making CEO in just two years, climbing to the top at Interfip Bolsa, then Peru's most profitable brokerage house. Recently, he jumped to become COO of the $400-million Bahamian-based Interbank Overseas. At the same time, however, the Peruvian economic landscape that once looked so promising took a serious pounding. Says Caballero: "We've seen the Asian crisis, the Brazilian crisis, the Russian crisis, El Niño, and now this."

"This" is the resignation of Alberto Fujimori, Peru's once-popular president, who succumbed to scandal. Growing distrust of the government propelled the markets into a sell-off and had foreign investors sprinting for the hills. "Right now," Caballero says with a laugh, "I kind of feel like I should have stayed in the U.S."

Like many who return home, Caballero succeeded by learning to apply the parts of his training that could be generalized and to ignore the specifics that couldn't. "Human resources, operations, corporate strategy, and the teamwork experiences are the courses you find yourself applying daily," he says, recalling corporate strategy meetings at Interfip Bolsa where he passed around copies of his B-school readings. But there were plenty of readings that didn't get handed out: "Most of the technical training didn't really apply," Caballero says. "For instance, we have no futures markets, and no options markets." (That fact still troubles him on a daily basis: "How do you hedge if you have no options market?" he asks. "You can't. So if something goes wrong, I'm dead.")

Then there was the matter of his personal business style, which had become more aggressive during business school. "Peruvian business culture is very soft. You never say things directly. When I first got to the U.S., I took six minutes to get to my point and would explain everything along the way." Upon his return to Lima, of course, the opposite problem surfaced: He'd become too direct. Colleagues found his straight-to-the-point way of speaking offensive. Shooting the breeze with a reporter in the middle of a frantic workday, Caballero seems to have returned to his Peruvian roots.

Ironically, Caballero says, the country's turmoil has been good for business. At least in the short term. "People are selling their stocks, and I'm making my fees," he said during the closing days of his tenure at Interfip Bolsa. "But in the long term we will need buyers, which means we have to cut costs. In the next few days our firm will lay off 30 percent of its workforce." His larger take on the crisis, however, reflects a faith that has not been required here since the Carter era. "It will be difficult," he says, "but we'll get over this. This won't last ten years. It will last a half year."

Edgar Nyamupingidza, University of Minnesota's Carlson School '95, Harare, Zimbabwe

It was a hell of a day in Harare. The cell-phone connections were unpredictable at best, the lines at the gas station were disturbingly long, and the e-mail never did work. He may have a maid, an Acura, and a nice place outside of Zimbabwe's capital, but you get the sense that things aren't going as smoothly for Edgar Nyamupingidza (NYAH-moopin-gidza) as they were two years ago during his stint at a small hedge fund in the quiet, white-bread Minneapolis suburbs. Back then, as a trading assistant fresh out of the Carlson School, he was taking home about $50,000 before bonuses. "A little on the low side," as he remembers it, but the pay wasn't bad for the Twin Cities, and he was in line for a more lucrative full-analyst job in a few months. There was just one hitch: His wife's company wanted her back in Zimbabwe.

The funny thing about forks in the road is the way they can seem like simple detours at the time. Planning to return to Minneapolis in a matter of a few months, Nyamupingidza packed his bags, persuaded his employer to hold his job, and landed in a nation sliding from bad to worse. But not long after he arrived in Africa, his American employer went under, taking his prized work visa with it. Since then, inflation in Zimbabwe has hit 70 percent, severe fuel shortages have become the rule, the nation has entered a costly war, misrule and corruption have crippled the ability of the government to lead, and the farming industry his wife returned to help has fallen subject to a government-sanctioned take-over by squatters.

Nyamupingidza quickly found that the sophisticated financial-service skills he learned in the United States placed him in a category of his own in Harare. Yes, they've made him something of a star at each bank where he's worked, but they've also turned out to be a personal burden. "When you return home, it can be frustrating if you have grand ideas about how to improve things," he explains. "You quickly find that the innovations you suggest aren't always valued, and the fact that you even suggest them leads some people not to trust you."

Lesson one came while trying to persuade an early employer to consider total return swaps as a safe and simple way to diversify holdings. "Instead of asking how it would help the client, the bank only wanted to know, 'Does it help us?'" he remembers. The reason: "Here, once you have money, it's been fairly easy to make more without applying yourself," he explains, "so the market kind of breeds people to be lazy." And so it turns out that the very things that make him more valuable in Zimbabwe also feed his disappointment.

All of which leaves Nyamupingidza rather conflicted. Should the downward economic spiral continue, he says he might consider cashing in his chips, polishing up his resumé, and heading back to the United States. And yet, he is also keenly aware of how much his training could help Zimbabwe. "My country is now like America was before the Great Depression," he explains. "We have slipped into a hyperinflationary environment, and we have never had this experience before." With his high-impact job as manager of product development and special projects at Kingdom Merchant Bank Limited, he realizes that he's in a position where he could make a difference. And that's hard to walk away from.

Sharifah Yuhaniz, University of Michigan '00, Kuala Lumpur, Malaysia

Kuala Lumpur's Petronas Twin Towers, the tallest buildings in the world, served as the windswept backdrop for the high-flying bank-robbery film *Entrapment*. But they're also an apt metaphor for the choice Sharifah Yuhaniz made when she left the United States for a position with McKinsey & Co.'s Southeast Asian operations. "It's a first-world experience set in the middle of a developing country," says Yuhaniz, a soft-spoken twenty-eight-year-old whose fifty-seventh-floor office has not insulated her from the street-level realities of consulting in Asia after the Crisis.

For Yuhaniz, staying in the United States after graduation was never an option. When her husband was transferred from Malaysia to Europe for a two-year assignment, she decided to use the time to grab an MBA. "But even without my strong family ties I would definitely have wanted to come back," she says. "After all, my competitive advantage is here. I understand Western concepts, but also the Asian way, and I feel that makes me much more marketable."

Bridging East and West has taken on an urgency in the years since Asia's economy cooled off. With many formerly publicly controlled monopolies now facing competition for the first time, Yuhaniz's return to Malaysia has meant far better assignments than she would have received working at McKinsey back in the States. "The economic situation has meant a tremendous amount of opportunity," she says. "It's given rise to the need for high-quality consulting. Every study you do here is strategic. You're giving CEO-level advice about the choices a company will make versus, say, studying a product launch, which is what I'd probably be doing in the U.S."

The rules of business have changed dramatically, as well. "Everybody here now acknowledges the need for clarity in communication," she says. "There's more acceptance not only of the need to be competitive in a Western sense but for true competence as opposed to just relying on social connections. Today, people are less likely to sweep things under the rug." All of which are positives for an MBA fresh from America. But when it comes to giving a company a piece of bad news, the messenger still has to do it in a culturally sensitive fashion. "In Asia you can't put someone on the spot and make him lose face," says Yuhaniz. "In America it's easy to say, 'Hey, I'm just being frank,' but here you need to deliver the news carefully, otherwise they'll consider you a bad guy and won't implement your recommendations."

Though she dismisses Asia's reputation for having a sexist business culture, being a woman charged with fixing broken companies only adds to the Western-seeming nature of her advice. Being a Muslim in the predominately Islamic nation of Malaysia often buffers that perception—though it did compromise her avenues for socializing while she was a student in the States. "A lot of the time, everybody would go for a drink after a study meeting," remembers Yuhaniz, who as a practicing Muslim does not consume alcohol. "If it was a big group, I'd go along and just not drink. But otherwise, I had to find other ways to experience American culture. Let's just say I went to a lot of football games," she remembers with a laugh. "Fortunately, Michigan had a good team."

Subodh Maskara, Kellogg '94, Mumbai, India

Among the lessons that Subodh Maskara didn't learn at Kellogg was how to deal with corruption. "In India you are constantly tested," says the thirty-four-year-old Maskara, who runs both UthPlanet.com and Maskara Industries Limited, two companies collectively valued at $30 million. "You figure out early on that to survive you have to 'manage your environment.'"

As evidence, he offers a case study of his own: Maskara Industries, a polyester-recycling operation he founded, needed additional electricity to keep up with rising customer demand—each day without the added juice meant $2,000 in lost business. To get the electricity, he needed a permit, which could take six months to obtain. "But if I were to take care of certain interests of certain individuals," he says, "the sanction could be made in a week. And the cost would be a very insignificant percentage of the benefits that would accrue to the company."

Weighing the economics of graft wasn't something Maskara planned on doing when he graduated from Kellogg in '94. Like so many others in his class, he moved to New York and toiled on Wall Street (at Credit Suisse First Boston). But he quickly began to realize that at heart he was an entrepreneur and would never be able to work for anyone but himself. He also came to believe that while America held an advantage for those wishing to work for large multinationals, India offered far greater opportunities for small and medium-size businesses. Especially, he says, "given that I already had an established base in India—a home, a strong network, and the kind of access to important people that few people there have."

The result: His UthPlanet.com has become the most popular youth portal in India, with 250,000 registered users and the potential for millions more, should the crowded nation ever become fully wired. Maskara Industries, with annual sales of $20 million, may be less sexy but has a similarly appealing upside. While his ventures couldn't be more different from each other, both sprang from his B-school studies: an extensive education in the ways of the global economy, from Internet branding to raising capital from the debt and equity markets. "Most of the courses taught you to solve problems with methodologies, and methodologies, in my opinion, are transportable across regions," he says. "Other than the hardcore American stuff like corporate finance, most of the courses trained you to look at issues in a structured manner, like an engineering problem."

Of course, Maskara's time on Wall Street gives him an added edge when it comes to investment. "Options, futures, and derivatives trading have just started in India," he says. "And half of the CFOs in medium to small companies here do not understand them, whereas I have the advantage of being able to use them in my day-to-day business to hedge risks."

That said, he now sees that in the beginning he focused too much on his business model—a typically American way to proceed, he says, and a clear holdover from his years in the States. Lately, he's even starting to make peace with the Indian way of doing things—the system of back-scratching and favoritism, which initially made him very uncomfortable. "It doesn't matter how good your business model is in India; it will die if you do not manage your environment. In India taking the so-called MBA route," he says with resignation, "would be a surefire road to failure."

12

Getting Back to Business

∙∙

SO YOU'VE SURVIVED THE LATE-NIGHT DECISION TREES, THE ENDLESS COMPANY PRESENTATIONS, THE GRUELING INTERVIEW PROCESS—AND FINALLY YOU'VE MADE IT. YOU'VE LANDED THAT COVETED SPOT— whether it's a summer internship or full-time post. But starting a new position is always a delicate dance. When you walk into your first job as an MBA, all eyes will be on you. Here, managing directors, senior VPs, and savvy associates reveal thirty-seven secrets to brandishing the confidence, wisdom, and polish of someone who has worked at a firm three years— even when you've only been there three weeks.

Secret number one: The thing nobody tells you about the honeymoon period is that there is no honeymoon period.

Four Ways to Win Over Colleagues

- It may sound harsh, it may sound Machiavellian, but the astute new associate never befriends the first people to seek him out. "There's a high probability they're desperately in need of instant allies," says Jim Poffley, a Wharton MBA who's now director of corporate relations at Penn State's Smeal College of Business Administration. Until you figure out who's in and who's out, be cordial and professional, but not

---

by David Blend, Anne Durham, Jacob Kalish, Maria Spinella, and Dirk Standen

chummy. If you find yourself the lunch pal of a guy who bad-mouths the managing directors, you become guilty by association.

- When your new colleagues ask about your background, mention past work experience first, then business school. By spinning your MBA as something that augmented an already strong business background—rather than trumpeting your degree as your biggest selling point—you'll let them know that you value time in the trenches as much as hours in the classroom.

- If one of your colleagues is doing a kick-ass job, tell the boss.

- The tasks may be routine and mind numbing, but delegating work in the first three months—before you know the skill sets of the people working with and for you—is risky, says one senior executive in the communications industry. Ultimately, it's your responsibility to get things done. And blaming a coworker for a screwup compounds the problem.

The Golden Mentor Rule

- From a Wall Street associate: "I once gave a brief presentation for the team I worked on. The vice chairman happened to walk in and later complimented me on my delivery. After that I began stopping by his office now and then with a good question. He and I struck up a great relationship, and he became my mentor. Now that I'm looking for a new position in the company, he's placing calls for me." The point: When the big guys toss even the tiniest crumb of attention your way, pounce on it like a starving dog.

Nine Things You've Got to Know About Face Time

- "Never pop into the boss's office at the end of the day with your coat on and briefcase in hand and ask if there's anything else you can do that night," says Kevin Berg, vice president in equity research at First Albany Corporation. "For the most part, you shouldn't leave the office before your boss." And certainly not with a transparently disingenuous offer of assistance.

- Don't thrust yourself in front of managers every time they hit the midnight coffeepot. It smacks of insecurity and sends the message that you think you should be judged on your hours rather than on work alone. Your superiors will be watching, so there's no need to point out that you are, in fact, in the office.

- That trick of leaving a message on a supervisor's voice mail and casually mentioning that it's 3:00 A.M.? Oldest one in the book.

- So don't use it more than twice.

- At night, it's okay to leave before a colleague. But as you stroll out the door, never cheerily say, "Don't work too hard," or you'll be branded as . . . the kind of jackass who says things like that.

- Managers notice when a new hire is putting in a lot of time, but they also notice if he's pale, flabby, and hasn't seen a movie since Bruce Willis had hair. "Some new employees get what I call office-itis," says Simon Canning, a managing director at UBS Warburg in New York. "You will be expected to put in an enormous amount of time, but you must find ways to relax, whether it's going to the gym for a couple of hours or taking vacation."

- What, exactly, does taking a vacation or working out tell your boss? That you have good time-management skills, understand how to prioritize, and know how to take care of yourself.

- That said, better not to utter the phrase "vacation day" for six months. Minimum.
- Oh, and, better not to utter the phrase "comp time" for, well, ever.

Four Keys to Nailing Your Assignments

- You don't need to gather every single scrap of information to make a decision. Collect as many of the facts as you can and form an opinion. "I've seen over-cautious new hires fall into the trap of waiting too long to take action," says Jeannine Haas, director of premium services in charge-card marketing at American Express. "You're not in a perfect world where you can always get all the information." Employ the 80-20 rule and move on.
- "When I first joined the company, I was hired into a stretch assignment," says Keisha McKenzie, an associate at J.P. Morgan Fleming Asset Management in New York. "I was so concerned about looking self-sufficient that I didn't ask for enough clarification. I ended up giving my manager only half of what he wanted." To avoid this, ask for a sample project from the past, one the boss loved.
- Most managers would rather you ask twenty questions when you first get the assignment than have holes to fill when you turn it in. Says J. Daniel Plants, a vice president of mergers and acquisitions at J.P. Morgan: "We don't want lone rangers who think they need to figure everything out on their own. In our business, that's a cultural defect. Answers lie within people, not books."
- The boss hands you the month's financials on Friday afternoon and requests a report on her desk first thing

Monday morning. You cancel your weekend plans, slave away for the next two days, and leave the report on her desk Sunday night. Tuesday afternoon, the report's still where you left it. What to do? Nothing. Don't ask if she's read the report. Don't ask if she has any questions. You did your job. You're a good soldier. That's what people will remember.

Two Tips for Traveling with the Boss

- When traveling with a manager, the wise associate will pack his pocket full of singles. He will be paying the cabdriver, tipping the bellhop, and picking up Cokes from the soda machine. Let the boss take care of any check presented in the presence of clients.
- From Franklin D. Mayers, vice president, MBA recruiting, at J.P. Morgan Private Banking: "If you have a trip coming up with a manager, take his assistant out for a drink. Stop by their office, and be straightforward. 'I'm traveling with Mr. Hammerschmidt next week, and I want to ask you about protocol.' The relaxed setting will allow you to learn how the manager acts, what he likes to drink, and what to expect during a typical day on the road."

Seven Communication Laws
You Better Not Break

- Know what you don't know. "When smart young people start a job, they want to impress you. So they talk a lot," says Scott Koppelman, a senior financial adviser at First Union Securities Financial Network in New York. "But actually, that's perceived as a negative. I'm looking for someone who's aggressive but who knows when to listen." Rule of thumb: Listen four times more than you talk.

- Treat your boss as if he were a client.
- E-mail is not a crutch, a wall to hide behind, or any other metaphor, for that matter. It should never be a substitute for dealing with a problem in person, says Cella Irvine, a Harvard MBA and former senior manager at an Internet company. By addressing the first rift that comes along face-to-face rather than from your PDA, you'll immediately establish yourself as someone who doesn't shy away from situations and has good interpersonal skills. Bothered by an assistant's sloppiness? An associate's wisecrack? Tell them politely and forthrightly. Using your mouth. Otherwise, you'll be pegged as an e-mail coward.
- Don't talk business in the bathroom. It puts people in the awkward spot of having to agree with you because they don't want to prolong the conversation. Managers tend to resent being put in an awkward spot. They're funny like that.
- When your boss calls you at home on a Saturday, speak as if you were sitting at your desk. Do not mention that you're taking something out of the oven or that the delivery guy is at the door.
- From a third-year associate at a bulge-bracket investment bank: "My firm has an open-door policy, which is great. But always pause for a moment before asking a senior person a question to make sure it's not something a peer could answer. A new hire who was junior to me once went straight to the director with a question I could have answered easily. He made us both look stupid."
- You're working with your boss on a project, and he's plumb wrong about something. "You have to tell him when no one else is around," says Jana Carlson, a professional recruiter at the Blackstone Group in New York. "'I think this number might be off. Do you want me to double-check it?' Pose it as a question, not as

'You're wrong.' Of course, you'd better be very sure
he's wrong."

How to Read the Tea Leaves

- The best way to find out what the company wants out
  of you is to look at who they're hiring. Are they strate-
  gists? Finance gurus? Image polishers? Says James Rice,
  a former senior VP at a Fort Wayne, Indiana, wire-and-
  cable manufacturing company: "When there's an opening in management, who they hire sends a strong
  message about the direction the company's going." It
  also tells you what kind of perspective the company
  embraces.
- To get a sense of what the brass values, look up their
  names at www.publicdisclosure.org. This site provides
  the names and cities—and, often, the employers—of
  people who have contributed to political campaigns or
  political action committees going back to 1980. Political leanings can be a bellwether of someone's ideals,
  hot-button issues, and, quite possibly, management
  style.
- It may take a bit of schmoozing, but it's worth asking
  your new boss what his favorite books are. Read them.
  It's a form of due diligence on the character, philosophy, and weltanschauung of the person with whom
  you'll soon be spending most of your waking life.

Three Rules for the Client Meeting

- When you're talking to a client, use first-person plu-
  ral. You are the company, and the company is you.
  Says Kevin McGowan, a principal at A.T. Kearney in
  Chicago: "Sometimes I hear new people say, 'Oh, I
  did this, or I did that.' We take them aside pretty
  quickly when they do that and remind them, 'Listen,

it's more of a we than an I.' The moment a client hires you, it becomes we. Always."

- After a meeting at the client's office, don't debrief until you leave the building. Even if there's no one else in the elevator.
- And that includes hand signals.

13

The Take-Away: Lessons from B-School's Best Minds

THEY LECTURE. THEY COLD CALL. THEY ASSIGN ENOUGH READINGS TO CHOKE A MOTHER HIPPO. AND FOR WHAT? WELL, THAT'S SIMPLE: TO ARM THEIR STUDENTS WITH AS MANY TOOLS AND AS MUCH INSIGHT AS they possibly can. But what if a professor could impart just one solitary nugget of information, a single gem that students would carry with them into the business world? What would it be? Here, nineteen of the country's top professors, from eight disciplines and eighteen schools, share the one thing they hope their students will remember after graduation. Feel free to take notes in the margins.

Prove Your Point

I know my students won't remember every formula, but I want them to remember this: There is no substitute for being able to convince people that your ideas are right, that your ideas are better. How do you do this? Part of it is knowing how to listen to people, part of it is knowing how to treat your peers well.

> —Bhaskaran Swaminathan, associate professor of finance, Johnson School, Cornell; Apple Award for Teaching Excellence, 1995 and 1998

by Russell Wild

Own the Rules

This is something all students should keep in mind, regardless of the field they enter. Successful businesspeople don't get sucked into playing other people's games—they grab hold of the game and make it theirs. Likewise, they aren't rushed into making hasty decisions—they operate on their own schedules. When it comes time to make a deal, they, not the other party, set the starting point for the negotiation.

—Karen Cates, assistant professor of management and organizations, Kellogg School, Northwestern University

Account for Everything

You've got to be able to put numbers in perspective. One of the crucial lessons of accounting is the true understanding of cost. Asking the cost of something—say, to manufacture a certain component—is a meaningless question unless you know what that something is going to be used for. For the same item, there can be many different costs, depending on whether the company intends to use it for pricing, performance measurement, or planning. Wise accounting can often spell the difference between a good business move and a poor one.

—Madhav Rajan, associate professor of accounting, Wharton School, University of Pennsylvania; David W. Hauck Award for Outstanding Teaching, 2000

Control What You Can

There's more to portfolio management than simply picking good stocks. Portfolio management is primarily about managing relationships. I want my students to learn to control what is within their control: the risks they bear, the fees they charge, and the services they provide. Excel in these dimensions, because even the best managers don't always enjoy superior performance.

—Charles M.C. Lee, director, Parker Center for Investment Research, Johnson School, Cornell; Apple Award for Teaching Excellence, 1997 and 2000

Cultivate Your Resources

HR is typically delegated to the lower levels of an organization, but if you look at successful businesses, you find effective HR policies and managers who use them strategically. People are key to a business. Whether it's entering new markets or boosting production, somebody has to deliver. A leader had better make sure her people are the right people, and that they have the right incentives.

—Stacey R. Kole, associate professor of economics and management, Simon School, University of Rochester; rated an outstanding teacher by *Business Week*, 1998

Focus on the Incentives

I don't care if my students remember facts. Any fact they learn today will be obsolete in ten years. I want them to be able to think like economists. That means understanding the incentives of all the relevant actors before making any strategic decision. If they're considering a merger, price cut, or new marketing campaign, they should take the time to really consider how the competitors, suppliers, and customers are likely to react.

—Michael Knetter, professor of international economics, Tuck School, Dartmouth; senior staff economist on President Clinton's Council of Economic Advisers

Outsmart the Computer

A student may be able to get an A in the classroom by memorizing a formula, but if he wants to succeed in business, he has to know why the equation works and when it can be applied. If a student's knowledge of a theory doesn't move from the abstract to the concrete, it's worthless. For instance, when a client asks a portfolio manager why he's buying certain stocks, the manager's got to have something tangible to back it up. Saying "Our computer models are showing that this stock is underperforming" simply isn't good enough.

—Gib Bassett, chairman, Department of Finance, University of Illinois— Chicago; Alumni Award for Teaching, 1997

Know Thy Customer

This is the bottom line: Customers fuel the business—any business. A deep understanding of the customer is critical in any marketplace. Who are the customers? Why will they buy? How will they evaluate the product? This sounds simple in practice, but very few businesses do it well.

—Barbara Bund, senior lecturer, marketing,
Sloan School, Massachusetts Institute of Technology

Don't Forget the Shareholders

Managers create value only when they do something for shareholders that shareholders cannot do for themselves. This is a key managerial responsibility. So when considering whether to allocate funds to a new venture, a manager should keep this in mind: Will the anticipated returns be greater than the returns that shareholders could get on their own in investments of similar risk level? If the answer is no, the manager has no good reason to proceed.

—Antonio Bernardo, assistant professor of finance,
Anderson School, UCLA; Citibank Excellence in Teaching Award, 1997

Open the Doors

Companies can use models to imitate everything from the financial markets to accounting practices, but they can't use a model to make people work together. You really have to listen to your coworkers and value their ideas. But listening isn't a technique; it's an attitude. That means managers must strive to show an active interest in employees, include colleagues in joint projects, and accept ideas from everyone.

—Roy J. Lewicki, professor of management and human resources,
Fisher College of Business, Ohio State University;
Dean's Distinguished Teacher

Do It Now

Execution is the key to effective performance. A rough but reasonable strategy well executed is much better than an extremely detailed, well thought out strategy executed poorly.

—Jennifer Chatman, professor of organizational behavior,
Haas School, University of California—Berkeley

Ignore Your Assumptions

The hardest thing for my students to grasp is that they are not the target market. Too often, people in business evaluate everything as if they were the consumer. My American MBAs couldn't come up with good ideas for selling tofu because they couldn't imagine that anyone actually eats the stuff. What's the answer? Spend time with the consumers of a particular product. Go to their homes; follow them around the grocery store.

—Thomas Gruca, associate professor of marketing,
Tippie College of Business, University of Iowa; rated an outstanding professor
by *Business Week's Guide to the Best Business Schools*, 1993, 1995, and 1999

Play the Game

No one likes competition, which is why most people and most organizations fight like crazy to get government to protect them from the vicissitudes of the market. Of course, government has its own pricing system for such protective services, and this is important for students to understand as they head into the hard, cruel world of organizational management. Government is neither the foe of business nor the archangel of the poor. State intervention is simply a tool that organized interests use to their own advantage. Those managers who best understand how to use the tool can do the most service for their organizations.

—Raymond D. Horton, chair, Department of Management; director, public and
nonprofit management program, Columbia Business School

Listen to the Market

I would hope that students remember just how powerful financial markets are. They reveal more than simply where to find the highest returns on investment—they act as a great mechanism for testing ideas and judging managerial effort. For example, when a manager of a public company announces a major policy change or plans for a new venture, the stock price will move in response. A smart manager will observe that movement and use it as very important feedback from investors in deciding how to proceed.

—Richard C. Green, professor of management and economics,
Carnegie Mellon; editor, *Journal of Finance*

Measure the Risks

I always start off my valuations class with the same quote: "If you're going to be a lemming, at least be a lemming with a life vest." What I mean is, if you can't fight the herd—and I believe going with the herd is in the human spirit—then learn the tools of valuation. So if you feel you must follow the herd and dump money into, say, the latest dot-com, you'll be doing it with a sense of the dangers involved.

—Aswath Damodaran, associate professor of finance, Stern School,
New York University; Professor of the Year Award, four-time recipient

Give the People What They Want

I can't stress this enough: People don't buy products or services. They buy solutions to painful problems. If your customer has a headache, sell aspirin, not vitamins.

—John N. Doggett, director, entrepreneurship programs for the Executive Education Division, McCombs School, University of Texas-Austin; top rating in *Business Week's Guide to the Best Business Schools*, 1995, 1997, and 1999

Take It Slow

Patience. Some graduates are so anxious to move up the ladder that they leave jobs before they've gotten the most out of them. For example, students who come to business school with a strong quantitative background think they're ready to work on $100-million portfolios. While they probably can handle the quantitative aspects, without experience they have no understanding of how to gauge a client's behavior and risk tolerance. Without that, they can't succeed. It won't take fifteen years to develop those skills, but it also won't take a day.

**—Mike Page, professor of finance,
Erasmus University's Rotterdam School of Management**

Make Strong Connections

In today's quickly changing business environment, digital organizations require leaders who connect people to the company and to one another. In the accelerated and condensed digital environment, leaders who can build strong relationships with a variety of people are the ones who will thrive.

**—Celia Virginia Harquail, assistant professor of business administration,
Darden School, University of Virginia**

Dig for Truth

I want my students to take everything they read or hear—such as the latest media buzz, or the "word from experts"—and really analyze it. Lots of things look good on the surface, but a bundle can be saved with just a little digging. When, for instance, Amazon's stock fell through the floor, it suddenly dawned on investors that the company was essentially a retailer. Well, hey, what did they want it to be? Had they stopped and taken the time to piece together the facts, they might have saved a bundle.

**—Dan Smith, chair of the MBA program and professor of marketing,
The Kelley School, Indiana University; top rating by *Business Week***

EIGHT THINGS THAT ARE *NOT QUITE* AS IMPORTANT TO REMEMBER

1. There's no "I" in team, but you can definitely get "me." And if you really scramble it, you're looking at "meat."
2. To make a term paper seem longer, write a heading with name, date, professor, class, social security number, and astrological sign.
3. There are no wrong answers. Only stupid ones, which pretty much guarantee you an inferior grade and ruin your future.
4. You know those name tags you get at recruiting events? In a pinch, you can effectively use one to pick your teeth.
5. Stalactites are the ones that hang down. Stalagmites are the other ones.
6. It's not necessarily a confirmed fact that one need pay a lot for a good muffler.
7. He who seeks only money is the poorest of all, but only in an abstract and fairly insignificant way.
8. Replacing the last syllable of a Jewish surname with the suffix "tron," "net," or "dom" results in a company name that sounds both aggressive and futuristic, e.g., Rosentron, Goldnet, Silverdom.

---

by Justin Heimberg

Epilogue:
How to Blow Off
Steam—A Primer

There's an old saying: Spreadsheets, strategies, and statistics make Jack a dull boy. Life for the typical MBA student is five parts study to one part fun. Not the finding-accounting-errors-in-the-Harvard-cases kind of fun. Rather, it's the let-loose-with-your-buddies fun, or the jet-ski-off-the-coast-of-Vietnam fun. Loading up a backpack and storing away the laptop for weeks, even months, has become almost a rite of passage for full-time MBAs. One recent grad explained his own adventures this way: "It's the last time until I'm filthy rich in retirement that I'll have two months with no obligations to travel around Asia or to take a cooking class in Paris." Below are stories of MBAs past and present who pursued the nonbusiness side of things as vigorously as they crunched the numbers.

Goal Oriented

For spring break of my first year, twelve of us chartered a fifty-eight-foot sailboat in Tortola for two weeks—beautiful weather the entire time, scuba diving, windsurfing, rum, card playing. The good thing about Tuck having trimesters is that we weren't in the middle of a term, so we were generally free from the burdens of B-school. The only thing we had to do for the following term was read The Goal. We had a competition to see who could have a picture taken reading it in the strangest place.

—ELIZABETH, TUCK '96

Kids' Stuff

*During our second year, a group of us coached kids at a local grade
school. The state of California had canceled phys-ed classes in the local
public schools. So we volunteered to coach fourth, fifth, and sixth
graders once a week. We tried everything—hoops, soccer, volleyball,
modern dance, gymnastics. The kids loved some things and hated others.
But they appreciated that we gave them a chance. That good feeling
would linger for hours.*

—MATT, STANFORD '96

Party of Fore

*During the summer between years one and two, a few friends and I
headed to Scotland for twelve days of golf. We figured, when else can
four buddies find time do this? We made the right move. It was awesome.
We sometimes played two rounds a day, which was helped out by the
long Scottish summer days. We started each morning with a huge breakfast and ended with a superb dinner, usually capped off with a cigar.*

—THOMAS, NORTHEASTERN '95

The Full Package

*I spent the summer after B-school pursuing the things I'd always wanted
to do. I traveled to Africa with seventeen of my B-school friends and
climbed Mount Kilimanjaro. I volunteered with a group in New York
and acted as a big brother to a young kid in grade school. I got involved
in local political races. I traveled through Europe and to the Middle
East. I went skydiving for the first time, and I studied Russian. I also
went to golf camp in New Hampshire.*

—DAVID, NYU STERN '98

Five-Card Studs

*One guy in my class organized a weekly poker game at his apartment. It
started out with four of us, but grew so that by the end of the year, ten
to fifteen people would come by during the course of the evening, which
often lasted until 3 A.M. As time went on, the stakes got higher—
$200–$300 pots were frequent.*

—TED, NYU STERN '98

Borderline Adventure

During Christmas break of my second year, I took off for a month to Asia. I figured the new millennium, one more term to go, I'm in the home stretch of B-school. Why not? I spent days exploring the lost city of Petra—the setting for Indiana Jones. I spent Christmas Day riding a camel on the India-Pakistan border. New Year's Day I watched the sun come up over palm trees and bamboo groves and pristine beaches of Goa in southern India. It was the perfect release from a torturous term, and it prepared me wonderfully for the one that followed.

—JAMES, NYU STERN '00

Best Friends' Wedding

Just after classes ended after my second year, but before graduation, I flew to Italy to attend the wedding of two B-school friends. It was a great event—the ceremony taking place in an old open-air rustic church overlooking the small town of Orvieto, forty minutes from Rome. The reception was amazing, the food fabulous, the wine outstanding. A few friends and I toured the Italian countryside before heading back home to receive our diplomas.

—JOHN, CORNELL'S JOHNSON SCHOOL '99

Pleasurable Business

I have a strong interest in international business, so during one winter break, I took a trip to South Africa, which was a great balance of business and pleasure. A recent alum working in Johannesburg was able to get us access to some great companies. The cultural aspect of seeing how things work in the most financially developed country in Africa, while learning about my own heritage, was both educationally enriching and personally rewarding. It wasn't inexpensive, but I wasn't really concerned about the cost—I knew that my upcoming signing bonus and salary would more than pay for the trip.

—ERIC, NYU STERN '98

It's a Small World

I looked at my time at B-school as not only an opportunity to learn but as a chance to see the world. In less than two years, I did everything from weekend trips to California to extended safaris in Africa. My fa-

vorite experiences were: chartering a yacht with friends in the Galapagos; hiking, camping, and white-water rafting in Costa Rica; traveling to Amsterdam and Israel; a three-day scuba expedition in Zanzibar with my father; and a two-month postgraduation trip to Asia with four classmates, including stays in Vietnam, Indonesia, Cambodia, Laos, and Thailand.

—JON, NYU STERN '98

One Step at a Time

I backpacked across Africa for over three months, camping and traveling overland from Cape Town to Nairobi. I rafted the treacherous Zambezi River, toured fabulous game parks, waking to the sounds of elephants and hippos at the foot of my tent. I detoured through Amsterdam, allowing a few weeks to chill out in Europe before starting work.

—BETH, UC–BERKELEY–HAAS '99

Southern Tour

I traveled to South America. I worked on a volunteer project for Conservation International in Bolivia, then I did the Inca trail in Peru. Then I spent some time checking out San Francisco, where I'd be moving for my new job.

—STEVE, KELLOGG '99

Steamy Summer

A bunch of girlfriends and I took our signing bonuses and booked a trip to Southeast Asia. For five weeks we traveled through Vietnam, Cambodia, Hong Kong, and Bali. It was 120 degrees with ninety-degree humidity every day. I've never been so wet in my life!

—AMANDA, HARVARD '99

Racing to Paradise

I finished school in May and was starting work in July, so in June I did something I'd wanted to do for years—I got on a boat for the Newport-Bermuda sailboat race. It was five days getting there, two days drinking rum there, and another five days coming back. There was no phone, no e-mail, nothing to do but think about making the boat go faster.

—FRANK, KELLOGG '92

Last Hurrah

I went to Greece and Turkey. I went scuba diving and island-hopping in Asia. I spent some time traveling in Thailand. It was a good way to end two years of business school because I went with classmates. It was the last opportunity to do things together before we dispersed all over the world.

—LAURIE, KELLOGG '00

Going to America

Just before classes began, I went to the United States. I had never been to America before. I figured that since New York seems to be the center of the financial world that I should experience it firsthand before reading about financial models and talking to investment banks. Yes, I saw the Statue of Liberty, ate in great restaurants, and had a marvelous time. I also got to see some beautiful East Coast beaches.

—ELIZABETH, ROTTERDAM '98

On the Road

I was taking a job in New York after graduation. I knew I'd be traveling a lot once work started—by airplane of course. I'd always wanted to travel across the country by car, to see and to meet cool people. So that's what I did. A friend and I hopped in my car and took the northern route during the month of August, arriving in time to get an apartment and get ready to work.

—BILL, UCLA-ANDERSON '97

Appendix A

....

Business School Rankings: What's in a Number?

B-school ratings published by *Business Week, U.S. News & World Report, The Financial Times,* and others have become a critical compass for most prospective students. Application rates, job prospects, even administrators' careers are affected by the scores. But how useful are they? Are they a good indication of what school is right for you? And what's their impact on what actually goes on in the classroom? Even if you don't consult these lists when deciding where to apply, you can't escape them. A school's rise up the rankings attracts top applicants, which in turn pushes up average GMAT scores up and sends acceptance rates downward. A bump up the rankings ladder is also a financial boon to a school's endowment. But a slip in the standings can be devastating—the number and quality of applicants drop, student morale dips, and recruiters shy away. Shortly before the release of the 2000 *Business Week* rankings, *MBA Jungle* assembled a panel to discuss the rankings' benefits, shortcomings, and continuing relevance to applicants, students, and employers. This transcript of the conversation will help you sort out these issues for yourself.

THE PARTICIPANTS

Jessica Portner   *MBA Jungle*

Michael Barclay   Finance professor at the University of Rochester's Simon School of Business. In 1994, Barclay was named to a *Business Week* list of the most popular B-school professors. Simon was ranked 21st this year.

Elizabeth Gabbay   Director of MBA recruiting for Scient, an Internet consulting firm.

Mary Giannini   Director of campus recruiting of the tri-state region for Deloitte & Touche.

Tracy Lloyd-McRae   A 2000 graduate of Georgetown University's McDonough School, ranked 26th.

Jennifer Merritt   The editor in charge of the rankings issue for *Business Week*. The 2000 rankings are the first she's overseen.

Jonathan Shapiro   A 2001 graduate from the University of Pennsylvania's Wharton School of Business, ranked first by *Business Week*.

Fallaw Sowell   Director of the MBA program at Carnegie Mellon University, ranked 14th.

Robert J. Swieringa   Dean of Cornell University's Johnson School of Management. Cornell dropped to 18th in *Business Week's* 1996 rankings, then bounced to 8th, where it has remained since 1998.

Joe Tracy   Vice president of the Federal Reserve Bank in New York and a former professor of economics at Yale and Columbia universities. In 1997, Tracy co-authored a study that was critical of rankings methodologies.

The Measure of All Things?

MBA Jungle: I'd like to begin by having Jennifer Merritt tell us a little bit of the history and rationale behind the rankings.

JENNIFER MERRITT: The rankings were started 12 years ago by John Byrne, a senior writer at *Business Week*. He thought the rankings that were out there were inadequate because they largely relied on test scores, yields, GPAs, etc. He didn't think that was a good measure of whether a business school was doing its job. He felt the only way to truly measure a school was by talking to its customers—recruiters, and students in their graduation year.

MBA Jungle: Mr. Tracy, you co-authored a paper that was critical of rankings methodology. Tell us about your paper and its findings.

JOE TRACY: The work was done jointly with Joel Walford while we were both at Yale. Joel is now at Wharton and I'm at the Federal Reserve Bank. It was a nontraditional research topic for two economists, and it came about mainly because our office was down the street from the Yale School of Management. We sensed the trepidation each time the administration waited for the rankings to come out. Since we were both educators, we cared very much about the learning—what actually takes place once students are there. We decided to determine whether the rankings reflected the value added by the education, or whether they were more a measure of the students the program attracted. In other words, did they reward the schools that educated most effectively, or just the ones that admitted the brightest students?

The result was that both the *Business Week* and the *U.S. News & World Report* rankings were more closely related to the quality of the students coming in than to our measure of the value added.

MERRITT: I'm curious about that, because the one thing *Business Week* really focuses on, which will often send schools up or down, is the quality of teaching, and whether students feel they're getting from their education what they need in the real world, which I would think is a value added.

JONATHAN SHAPIRO: But a lot depends on when you ask. I just finished Year One a couple of months ago. Before I started my summer internship, I would have said, "You know, a lot of the classes we're taking aren't responding to the changing economy."

Right now, I'm working in an Internet group, and I'm spending my time writing about supply-chain management and marketing-program mixes. So if you asked me now, I'd say, "Yes, the classes were great preparation." Next June, right after I graduate, I may have another answer in terms of the added value I got from the program. Maybe it would be better to ask students three years later, rather than right after graduation, as they're about to leave for, you know, a trip around the world.

MERRITT: This is something that comes up a lot actually—when to measure? But with the graduates' having so much more work experience when they go in—an average of five years—we feel we can be confident in their responses about what they're learning. Also, the recruiters have experience with many schools over time.

TRACY: Recruiters do have several schools where they interview, so they can make direct comparisons. The concern Joel and I had about asking students—really at any point—is that in most cases they've gone to one business school. Yet you're asking them, in effect, to make a comparison across a set of schools.

Sudden Impact

MBA JUNGLE: What do the rankings mean to each of you? What kind of impact do they have on students—and prospective students?

TRACY LLOYD-McRAE: I definitely looked at the rankings. I know my classmates did, too. And we watch them. In an ideal world you want people first to think about what they want out of an MBA and look at the different programs and try to ask, "Is this the right city for me and for the career that I'm in?" and then use the rankings as a tool to find a school that's the right fit. Georgetown's ranked, I think, 25th or 26th by *Business Week*, so we see it as a challenge. The faculty and administration are doing a lot because they know we watch the rankings, and that recruiters do as well.

MARY GIANNINI: From a recruiter's perspective, I think we need to have a strong sense of the competencies and skill sets that we're looking for. You may not get what you need out of the top five schools, given the particular slant of the curriculum, where the students want to go after they graduate, etc. I've always been a real believer in the idea that first you should take a look at what kinds of core competencies and specific skills you need, and *then* you go and see where that fit is.

For example, there's a small program at SUNY–Albany, which is basically a regional MBA program. I don't even know if it's ranked at all. Yet if you're looking for someone with a concentration in human-resource information systems, which is a very niche-type program, they probably have the best one around. I've worked for two firms that do consulting for our clients on this very issue, so you bet we go up there. Now, do we look for people in their finance program? No.

ELIZABETH GABBAY: At Scient, we're in a very interesting position. We're only two and a half years old, and we're just starting to populate the company with MBAs. This is going to be a pivotal year for recruiting because we've just exploded—our MBA recruiting targets have quadrupled from last year. But we don't really have a benchmark yet as to what will be successful, which is why I think the rankings will be a very interesting tool for us. When I was at Andersen Consulting, there was a commitment there to using the rankings and hiring from the business schools that they were comfortable with. That made it a little easier to do recruiting, of course, but you were sort of locked into and very driven by the rankings.

MBA JUNGLE: Dean Swieringa, when you came to Cornell in 1997, to what extent did you use the rankings to identify those areas you might improve upon?

ROBERT J. SWIERINGA: I won't downplay the role that the rankings had in 1996, when the school dropped dramatically. In many ways that was a wake-up call, and the school, the students, and the faculty realized that they were in a very competitive world. They really had to sit back and think about what they wanted to be in the future and what kinds of investments they were willing to make.

MICHAEL BARCLAY: As a professor, it's been my experience that the rankings have had a very dramatic effect on what happens in the classroom. Some of the changes have been very good for students; others not as good. There's intense competition among business schools to make students happy these days: We're going to put a lot of effort into our teaching. We're going to make sure that our lectures are well prepared and organized. We're going to use computer-generated graphics. We're going to try to put you in a building that's comfortable, has state-of-the-art facilities, good acoustics, and sight lines and everything else.

But if there's a downside to the competition to make students happy, it's this: Students are very good at judging the style of the presentation in the classroom; but at that stage in their career they're not in the best position to judge the *content* of what's delivered. And I think there's been a disturbing trend in business schools over the last 10 years or so in that part of the product has gotten watered down.

Rather than pushing students to do difficult analytical material, and making them struggle with that, sometimes the instructor will say, "Well, let me give them a little bit of intuition and we can talk about the problem and think about what the solution would look like. They'll be happier. I'll be happier. My teacher rankings will go up. Everything will look good."

I think at the Simon School the students have benefited from the rankings because we've put a lot of effort into our teaching, and we have the checks and balances in place to make sure our program is as rigorous and challenging as possible. And we're going to do that regardless of how it affects the survey. I'm not convinced every other top business school can make that claim.

SWIERINGA: I don't necessarily accept the premise that academic standards are dropping. Some of our most demanding courses are taught by our most effective teachers, in terms of the kinds of evaluations they're given. Any change in style at Cornell is really being brought about by the marketplace. Students are different today. They have an experience base that's quite different than what we had years ago. We're trying to draw out that experience and take advantage of it in the classroom. There's more pressure on the professor to try to indicate the relevance of what's being taught.

BARCLAY: I certainly agree that the best teachers at any university are also going to be delivering the high-quality, rigorous content, and, you know, I don't want to push this panic button about the demise of MBA education. I think the quality of education is still very high in almost every business school, but it has changed.

For example, there's this currently fashionable notion of "hitting the ground running" when you get to your job. That concept can be overdone, because there's a fundamental difference between training you for your next job and providing you with an education that's going to be valuable throughout your career. Of course, it would be very easy for us to train the students to do their next job. But we really have to think about all the skills a person needs in order to have a successful career. What we'd like to do is specialize in the broad, general education that's going to set the student up for a very successful long-term career path.

SWIERINGA: But I don't think it's a choice between less filling and tastes great. Let me give you an example. We have the Parker Center, an electronic platform with a group of professors—Charles Lee, Swaminathan, and others—who teach a very analytical approach to the analysis of financial statements and financial information. The electronic platform allows us to teach courses in analysis, building portfolios, doing modeling exercises, and so forth using point-and-click technology. We have data feeds—we can follow 14,000 U.S. companies and 85,000 international companies, almost all with point-and-click technology. So our students can learn how to implement and to make the choices that are guided by the analytics. It's not one versus the other.

FALLAW SOWELL: It's a subtle point, but I think where you may be seeing the softening of the business school curriculum is in the required courses. Absolutely the electives are rigorous and demanding, but the students are the ones deciding whether or not they actually take those classes. So what you're seeing is a softer side on the required courses that everybody has to take. That's what goes on. Again, this may be just the result of heterogeneity in the student body. It may not be a dumbing down as much as adjusting for a different audience.

Playing Hardball

LLOYD-MCRAE: I think it's important that professors be responsive without dropping the quality. And that's really not easy to do when you've got students who are bleary-eyed and complaining. At Georgetown, we went from a traditional schedule to six-week modules, so that we now have 10 classes a semester. This was after the faculty and administration analyzed other MBA programs. But when they made the change the first time, with our class, it was grueling. The professors wanted to know what we thought: "Okay, this is the first time we're doing this so we need your feedback." And we're like, "We're not getting sleep."

Some of the professors said, "You're not supposed to sleep. This is MBA school." Others listened and adjusted, and it was still rigorous. The good professors, the ones we rank well, listen, laugh at us, and adjust where they can; but at the end of the class, when we've gotten some sleep, we wake up and think, "You know, I really learned something."

SHAPIRO: There are professors, I'm sure, who go too far and say, "Okay, instead of running all the numbers on this case, I'm going to make your life easier and force-feed you some of the answers."

BARCLAY: That's a good example, because the way a case is going to work most beneficially is if the students take that mass of details—some relevant, some irrelevant—and just kind of barrel through that and try to figure out what are the most important points. If you want students to do that, it takes training. The easiest thing for the instructor to do is say, "Okay, now you've all read the case and you've all thought about it, now how about this for an answer?" We'd go through and blah, blah, blah, and everybody says, "Oh yes, that would be great."
On the other hand, what you've just trained the student to do is read the case, think about what was in there, and then come out prepared to *listen* to the answer. And that's a much different process than training the student to say, "Let's struggle with this case for however many hours it takes so that when I'm done I'm confident that I have the right answer."

LLOYD-MCRAE: I think that the kind of students who are attracted to the top business schools are not looking for that. Sure, you may hear them complain about the workload; they may be ticked off that they can't eat a meal at home; but if you did it the easy way, the school would be penalized. The students would say, "This is not what I'm paying for." In the end, they're very discerning customers.

SHAPIRO: Darden, at the University of Virginia, jumped up a number of notches a few years ago largely because of the rigorousness of the course load. At the very end, though, you add those last couple of pieces that push people over the edge. You know, "Before, I could stay up really late and research companies that I wanted to interview with, and now I can't even do that anymore. And now I'm at a real disadvantage." And so the school shot up in the rankings but then slumped back down.

LLOYD-MCRAE: You go to Darden because you want that rigorous education. You know you're not going to sleep, but they saw that students appreciated that. The problem is, the administration responded by making it even tougher. They piled on too much, so the students didn't even have time to look for jobs. When recruiters came, they felt discombobulated because nobody was prepared for interviews. And that doesn't reflect the quality of the students.

GIANNINI: No—I think there's a balance here, and obviously they're not balanced anymore. Why do people go to business school? I don't think they go because it's some kind of intellectual exercise. They go because it's going to improve their career opportunities. If you damage that piece of why they're going, you're not meeting the needs of the students. I've recruited at Darden, and, I mean, they walk in and they're zombies.

SHAPIRO: There's no one from Darden here to defend it, so I will, I guess. I have friends from Darden who'll say, "It's the best preparation, and yes, I crashed while I was there, but it was well worth it." I also know people who've said, "I didn't need to go through all of that."

Falling from Grace

SOWELL: All of the schools have responded to the rankings. A great change has been taking place in business school education. The quality of students has gone up dramatically. The quality of education has gone up dramatically. But when you go in and do a ranking, a top 20, and you force this curve, what you miss is the wonderful improvement that's taking place in this industry. It's the equivalent of everybody scoring above 90 on the exam and someone saying, "Well, sorry you got that 91. You get a C." In the end, they're giving a failing grade to some people by forcing a rankings curve.

MERRITT: You mean improvement based on starting salaries or—I'm unclear where this comes from.

SOWELL: We can certainly look at salary. We can look at GMAT scores and other things. What a ranking misses is the overall quality improvement that's been taking place over time. People think, well, if you drop four rankings, then you must be doing something wrong. Everybody is just doing great stuff and that gets missed when we start getting down to second-guessing—you know, "They dropped two spots."

TRACY: Look at GMAT scores [which *U.S. News* uses in its rankings, but *Business Week* does not]. There's a huge improvement across the board. It's like the Olympics, where the difference between first place and 13th place in the 100-meter race is three-hundredths of a second.

BARCLAY: But does that mean that we've got a huge number of smarter people now? There are some schools that will say, "Go do the review course," and so people will take the GMAT multiple times. That's a good argument, in my mind, against rewarding schools in the rankings for having high GMAT scores.

MERRITT: And I'd be interested to see how important that is for the New Economy worker, anyway. I mean, I wonder what Bill Gates would have scored on his GMAT? In any event, we always point out that there's not a lot of difference between top schools. But I can reasonably say that there are some huge gaps overall, based on what students and recruiters are saying.

TRACY: I think, though, that even if you qualify the rankings, there's a false sense of precision. If we take the same school, take the same quality students, and run the whole year over again; bring in recruiters from the same campuses and then reinterview them; and do that 1,000 times, you're going to find that these rankings jump all over the place.

MERRITT: It's not perfect, but it's the best we feel we can come up with.

TRACY: Well, it's devastating if you fall out of the top 20.

MERRITT: Yes, there are schools out there that are using this in the wrong way. And I have no respect for them. They look at the rankings and say, "Oh, my God, we have to get up in the rankings. What do we have to do? Well, you're fired and we're doing this." That response is such a disservice to the students. And you know what? Those schools often go down. You know who they are—everyone knows. I'll be the first to admit that this is not perfect. But we feel that if you look at the choices we have, this is the best way we've come up with.

MBA JUNGLE: At *Business Week*, do you ever feel responsible or do you ever cringe when you hear about people that are let go because the school went down in rankings?

MERRITT: I don't feel responsible for their being fired. I feel sorry for the school taking that tack. Every dean from probably the top 30 or 40 schools, sometimes even more, comes in to talk to me, and this is one thing I tell them: I feel extremely responsible for what happens, and therefore I am committed to doing this the best that I can. And so I hope that you use the rankings for good and not for evil. Maybe you totally ignore them, like Darden. They didn't totally ignore them, but to some of that stuff, they said, "You know what? That's too bad. This is what we are and this is what we offer."

Into the Future

MBA Jungle: Let's talk a bit about the future of the rankings. Are there ways you think the rankings could—or should—evolve?

Lloyd-McRae: I think the rankings could offer more information so they're not taken so literally. I think they're a necessary evil. They raise the standard by making us compete. We're getting a new building at Georgetown, and it's because the administration looked at other schools. The rankings encourage that.

But it would be nice if the rankings did have a much more detailed breakdown as to which schools do what best, and more about the culture. For example, in the survey I got, I had to write some things I thought were really important in the little comment box at the bottom. We had international residency required for all of our students. Now where do I put that in a survey? That was one of the highlights of my time at Georgetown.

Merritt: I don't know if you've seen our rankings book or the *Business Week* web site, but we put those there. We do try to break it down as much as possible, but in a magazine you have limited space.

Gabbay: Rankings are a valuable tool, but I think there's still something nebulous we'll never get from any ranking. We had a student, for example, who was very bright, from a top five school; and as time went on, we found that culturally this was somebody who was going to clash, so we retracted the offer. There are some things you can't capture in a survey.

Sowell: I think it will meet the needs of this industry better when we get away from rankings and into profiles. What seems to strike a chord is the idea of people using rankings to find the appropriate fit for them. Every school has its own personality, and when someone's looking to apply, they need to find out what's right for them given their background and aspirations. And a ranking doesn't necessarily do that, because it's just one measure that someone has written down. Some algorithm.

A student says, "Hey, I want to go to business school." That carries opportunity costs. She's walking away from her salary, spending on tuition, moving someplace, living. This is a huge expense. I know that numbers are appealing, but others are stepping into the marketplace, like the *Financial Times* Web site, where you can actually design your *own* rankings. This is how the industry is evolving, and, I think, should continue to evolve.

SWIERINGA: I don't know what the future is going to be like, but the business world is changing dramatically. We in academia have traditionally focused on accounting and finance and marketing, but increasingly the emphasis is on leadership, technology, globalization, and entrepreneurship. People coming to school now may also have experience in the New Economy. So I wonder if the role of the organizations that offer rankings will be in providing information and tools that will allow people to do the dynamic analysis you were describing.

MERRITT: One difference that I can see in future rankings is the addition of some kind of measure of the influence of a business school on the real world. We're struggling to figure out how that would work, but we think that's important. It would measure a little bit of innovation, a little bit of how a school is actually affecting the world around it—not just the world it's in.

BARCLAY: That's a little bit ironic, because we were talking earlier about how the rankings affect faculty members and what goes on in the classroom. And one of the traditional ways in which business schools have influenced the outside world is with their fundamental research. If you think about the finance area that I'm in, you don't have to go very far back to find things that revolutionized business practice—the Capital Asset Pricing Model, the Black-Scholes options-pricing model—and one of the things the rankings have done is to shift the set of resources in business schools away from fundamental research toward teaching, infrastructure, and technology. In the short run, all of those have been very good for students. I get concerned, though, that the shift is consuming our capital when we still need to understand the world better and change business practice.

TRACY: I think we've all agreed there's no ideal ranking. The real key is giving prospective students information and helping them process it. What was alarming to Joel and me when we started surveying schools was that there really is no standard for certain basic data items that every school agrees on. We'd get call-backs from schools saying, "Well, how do you want this number reported? We give it this way to this group, and other groups want it this way." That is very confusing to students, because then you're comparing apples and oranges.

BARCLAY: In the end, this whole thing boils down to supply and demand, right? If we could get all the students we wanted, then none of this would be an issue. We'd say, "I don't care what our ranking is."

Appendix B

....

Industry Guides

Below are guides to the nine industries targeted by most graduating MBAs. These brief reports provide an overview, expected salary and bonus information, and reports from insiders on the culture, the crowd, and the work environment. For a more in-depth look at a particular industry, scoot over to your school's career center or scour the Web at such sites as Wet Feet, Vault, and mbajungle.com.

CONSULTING

Overview

Consultants provide a wide range of services to businesses. They identify managerial and institutional problems, perform in-depth quantitative and qualitative analyses, recommend and develop solutions, and assist in implementation. Time-constrained senior management often relies on consultants to bring unbiased, outside perspectives to problem solving. A consultant's independence allows for enhanced access to information from internal sources, as well as from the competition.

Today there are more than 250,000 working consultants, creating revenue of approximately $60 billion a year. Recent economic developments and corporate trends have increased the number of consulting firms. Also, many companies are choosing to outsource activities previously performed internally. This trend, combined with corporate downsizing, has caused many former executives and recent B-school grads to join the ranks of consulting firms. The hefty paychecks and access to new, challenging opportunities don't hurt, either!

Major Players

The industry's elite includes Arthur D. Little (the founding father), A.T. Kearney, Bain & Co., Booz-Allen & Hamilton, McKinsey & Co., the Boston Consulting Group, and the Monitor Company.

The Big Five accounting firms (Arthur Andersen, Deloitte & Touche, Ernst & Young, KPMG, and PricewaterhouseCoopers) all have consulting arms. Many of those divisions, however, are separating from their parents. Andersen Consulting has officially split from Arthur Andersen and is now Accenture (Arthur Andersen also has its own management consulting business). Ernst & Young sold its consulting business to Cap Gemini. Information technology firms are multiplying rapidly at the moment. Some of the most prominent are American Management Systems, IBM Consulting, Computer Sciences Corporation, and Diamond Technology Partners.

The newest sector in the consulting industry is web strategy firms. Pioneers include Scient, Viant, Razorfish, Zefer, Organic, and Agency. com, though business in this sector fell off dramatically after so many dot-coms shut down.

Consulting revenues have increased more than 40 percent over the last two years and don't appear to be slowing down, with the estimated annual growth rate over the next two years at 15 percent. Depending on the MBA program, as much as 30 to 40 percent of MBAs enter this field. Most major consulting firms actively participate in both on- and off-campus recruiting.

Salary

Just out of business school, you can expect to make anywhere from $75,000 to $150,000. Most consulting firms offer from $100,000 to $120,000, which generally includes bonuses (20 to 50 percent of annual salary), and they offer additional perks like a company car. Senior managers make $200,000 to $250,000.

Hours

Generally, consultants' hours aren't nearly as grueling as those of investment bankers. About 60 hours a week is the norm, although some say they only work 45 to 50. Crunch periods can be more intense, with teams working 75 to 80 hours a week.

Travel

Most consultants travel about three to four days a week for a good part of the year. The typical schedule is Monday through Thursday at the client site and Friday in the home office. Of course, this can vary from project to project and firm to firm, and even within the same firm from office to office. We did talk to a few lucky consultants who only have to travel one or two days a week, or 25 to 30 percent of the time.

Office Culture

Collegial, friendly, and close-knit are terms that came up often in discussions of the atmosphere in this industry. Team bonding is an important part of most projects. As one senior manager explains, "You'll be spending 10 to 12 hours a day with these people. You want to get along."

Though a couple of conservative companies still cling to dark suits and ties, most consulting firms these days are "business casual" (lingo we've also heard includes "corporate casual" and "smart casual"). When on the client site (which for many consultants can be four or five days a week), however, the motto is, "We go by their rules."

The Crowd

In some areas, for instance, strategy, almost everyone has an MBA. Other sectors are more academically diverse. One associate at a management consulting firm says his colleagues come from "extremely diverse backgrounds—MBA, J.D., M.D., international degrees, Ph.D.s in everything from physics to literature." Another associate, at one of the industry's oldest and most elite firms, raves, "There is a fantastic diversity of backgrounds and previous work experience, which adds to the richness of team dynamics." She says that in addition to Harvard and Wharton B-school grads, her colleagues also include a "potpourri" of Ph.D.s, M.D.s, and J.D.s.

There are definitely more women in this industry than in banking or finance.

Getting In

Consulting firms recruit quite heavily on B-school campuses. *Jungle* spoke with many insiders who took this traditional route to get into the industry. Others networked their way to the position they wanted (particularly those interested in e-business or Internet-related jobs). All offered myriad tips on the best way to get your foot in the door.

- Don't cast your net too wide.
- Be familiar with the industry—talk to friends, set up informational interviews with recent grads, use your alumni base.

- Read *Consulting News, Consulting Magazine, Business Week, Industry Standard.*
- Hands-on experience is the best way to get an idea of what a particular firm is all about. Summer internships are competitive but can be invaluable opportunities.
- There are different kinds of consulting. Know the one you are interested in.

Resumé Tips

- Highlight leadership experiences (president of consulting club in B-school, etc.).
- Explain what you did to make an impact on a specific project, either in words or in dollars. Provide an example of the results.
- Highlight a global experience, "even if you only visited the Mexican plant for three days during a summer internship."
- Demonstrate technical knowledge and experience (even if it's only HTML, put it in).
- Include extracurricular activities. Charity and community work is a plus.
- Stress communication and interpersonal as well as analytical and research skills.
- Don't blow anything up into more than it is. Says one veteran, "It will come out during the interview and misrepresentation will surely kill you."
- Key words: *analyzed, managed, led, formulated, assessed.*

INVESTMENT BANKING

Overview

Investment banking (or I-banking) is, in fact, neither investing nor banking. Broadly, investment bankers work to raise capital and provide investment advice for the bank's clients. The industry breaks down into three main categories:

Corporate finance.   CorpFin, to those in the know, is the process of raising money for corporate clients; it lies at the core of the traditional investment bank.

Sales and trading.   This crew buys and sells securities and commodities in a high-pressure, market-driven culture.

Research. Analysts generally focus on either fixed income or equity. They work to predict the movement of specific stocks, and their advice is extremely powerful in the industry.

Major Players

Top-tier full-service firms include Merrill Lynch, Morgan Stanley Dean Witter, Goldman Sachs, Salomon Smith Barney, Lehman Brothers, Credit Suisse First Boston, and J.P. Morgan Chase, many of which are newly merged entities. For instance, Salomon Brothers and Smith Barney joined forces only recently. Credit Suisse First Boston forked over more than $11 billion to acquire Donaldson, Lufkin & Jenrette in 2000, and Chase and J.P. Morgan also tied the knot last year.

The repeal of the Glass-Steagall Act in 1999, a 1929 law created to separate commercial banking from investment banking, has also resulted in numerous mergers. Many smaller, regional I-banks have been acquired by commercial banks as a result. Hambrecht & Quist was acquired by Chase; Robertson Stephens was bought by Bank of America and then sold to BankBoston; and Alex Brown (the oldest investment bank in the United States) was acquired by Bankers Trust, which then merged with Deutsche Bank.

Salary

Packages for associates in the corporate finance area just out of B-school hover around $150,000. Vice presidents generally pull in about half a million a year. And if you make it to partner, you can expect to rake in several million at the top firms.

Sales and trading salaries start at about $75,000 for recent MBAs— plus about a $20,000 signing bonuses and a year-end bonus that could double the base salary.

Research analysts often earn more than those in other positions at investment banks. Their bonuses depend on the accuracy of their forecasts. Top analysts often win television, radio, and/or Internet gigs where they can make even more.

Hours

You make a ton of money in this business, but you'll be hard-pressed to find time to spend it. Most corporate finance MBAs average 80 to 100 hours a week during their few first years. Most insiders agree that you should be willing to put everything else in your life on hold.

Travel

Most I-banking jobs aren't travel intensive—except for the occasional client outing or industry conference. Some I-bankers are on the road one to three times a month, but never as much as consultants. There are always exceptions: One high-yield salesperson claims to be "on the road all the time."

Office Culture

The I-banking community is described by most insiders as "close-knit," most likely because employees eat, breathe, and sometimes sleep in the office. One associate attributes the bonding to the office space. I-bankers do leave the office from time to time—for happy hours and client dinners, excursions to sporting events, sailing trips, and more. Tip: Investing in golf clubs and lessons is probably a good idea.

Many firms on the Street are loosening up and have recently changed their dress code to business casual. Investment banking is still the most conservative of industries, though, and you should definitely have a few suits in your closet.

The Crowd

This industry is definitely not the most diverse. The atmosphere is "testosterone-charged," says one associate. Another admits that it is "mostly white-male-dominated" but adds that it is "getting better on this front."

Getting In

On-campus recruiting is the most common route to landing a job in this industry. However, if you have a nontraditional background, it can be tough to get an investment-bank position. Your best bet is probably in sales and trading.

The hiring process is exhausting, sometimes including as many as six rounds of interviews. This business requires endurance, as does its rigorous selection process. The interviews themselves can also be trying.

Veterans recommend doing your research before every interview. One even advised second-years to treat the process as they would a class and "study hard." Read recent articles and understand current conditions. Make sure the interviewer understands that you know a lot about the company and are ready to make a commitment. You should also be prepared for straightforward questions like "Why do you want to be an investment banker?" "What interests you about finance?" and "Why do you want to work for this bank in particular?"

Many emphasized the importance of understanding accounting. Said one recent hire into the industry: "I had to verbally construct a cash-flow statement." Case studies are also popular with I-banking inter-viewers as a tool to evaluate a candidate's quantitative and analytical skills.

MARKETING

Overview

MBAs may associate marketing with the ubiquitous four Ps—product, place, promotion, and price. Essentially, marketing links a firm to its customers by aligning the company's resources to meet customer needs. This process includes many phases, and a marketer can be anything from a salesperson to a strategy-shaper to a number cruncher.

Marketing-related jobs include the following:

Advertising.   Determining a promotional message and a channel to reach target customers.

Brand management.   Managing all aspects of marketing for consumer-packaged goods.

Competitive analysis.   Benchmarking the price, positioning, market share, or other metric against your competition.

Consumer research.   Determining the characteristics, trends, and needs of a given market.

Product management.   Managing all aspects of marketing and devel-opment for a product category, typically high-tech consumer products, content, or software.

Sales.   Generating transactions.

Major Players

Marketing's role differs from company to company. In the consumer-products industry, it plays a lead function, while in other sectors it may play a more supporting role. Arenas include:

Consumer products.   Unilever, SC Johnson Wax, Nabisco, Kraft.

Financial services.   American Express, Citibank, Merrill Lynch.

Professional services.   Consulting, legal, accounting, and investment banking (Deloitte Consulting, CSFB, Korn Ferry).

Pharmaceuticals.   Pfizer, GlaxoSmithKline, Bristol-Myers Squibb.

Entertainment and media.   Disney, AOL Time-Warner.

This industry is booming. Employment for marketing, advertising, and public relations managers is expected to rise faster than the average for all other occupations through 2006. MBAs are in a plum position because of their quantitative and communication skills. And there's good news on the salary front. Though the money in marketing still doesn't compare to that of investment banking, between January 1999 and 2000, average salaries for marketing graduates increased 11 percent.

Salaries

Associate brand/marketing managers (one to two years out of business school) can expect $75,000 to $100,000 a year.

Hours

Typically 50 to 60 hours per week, 60 to 70 during crunch periods.

Travel

As a general rule, travel is infrequent, about three to four times a year, usually domestic. One important exception is the international brand manager.

Office Culture

Of course, culture varies from company to company. One associate marketing manager describes her office as "moderately hierarchical, old-world corporate: Junior people are clustered in cubicles, while brand managers and above enjoy offices with windows." Another characterizes her office milieu as "open and informal." Socially, the teamwork involved in this industry encourages frequent interaction among colleagues. Company-sanctioned socializing is common.

The Crowd

MBAs in the marketing biz come from all walks of life—"engineers to advertising execs to environmentalists to salespeople." One senior analyst at a large high-tech corporation attests that "just about any background can be leveraged in some way. You don't have to be an expert in the marketplace, but you have to be able to learn quickly, turn information around, and be decisive." The male-female ratio in this industry is much more balanced than it is in many others (like investment banking). Women make up a large chunk of marketing majors at most B-schools.

Getting In

Most people we spoke to in the marketing industry were recruited on campus. Those who have changed jobs since B-school networked with peers from their MBA programs. They recommend identifying a contact and scheduling an informational interview. Use that connection to forward your resumé to the appropriate party rather than sending a blind resumé to human resources.

Be prepared for cases. Marketing firms are turning increasingly to the case-study method to test your analytical abilities and assess your marketing skills during the interview process. An example would be: "Polarama is a firm that markets children's toys with a North Pole theme. They are considering whether or not to introduce 'snow ball,' a new line of Beanie Baby-esque stuffed animals, in time for the holiday season. What would you recommend?" Be aware that interviewers are not only assessing the quality of your answer but are also looking for evidence of specific leadership skills.

MEDIA/ENTERTAINMENT

Overview

Those who work in the industry will find it's often a thrilling, if bumpy, ride. Jobs in these companies might not have the security or the salary of more traditional MBA-track positions, and the volatile economics of the industry keeps stress levels high. But the diehard media junkies who work in this field wouldn't have it any other way.

Aside from the obvious—working on the business side of a publishing house, film company, etc.—MBAs looking for exposure to the M&E industry can choose from a variety of positions, even without prior experience.

- *Consulting.* For those who would like to be near the industry but aren't willing to sacrifice the stability of a traditional MBA job, many top consulting firms have growing practices in M&E, including Booz-Allen & Hamilton, Pricewaterhouse Coopers, and McKinsey & Co.

- *Investment banking.* Opportunities abound in buy-side banking or asset management. For example, at a mutual fund you may develop relationships with M&E CFOs to try to decide whether you should buy into AOL Time-Warner or Disney.
- *Business development.* In-house posts developing strategic alliances and partnerships can be difficult to get directly out of B-school.

Major Players

The Telecommunications Act of 1996 enabled a host of new players to get into the game, as it allowed phone and utility companies, among others, to create and distribute entertainment content. Still, the dominant players are huge conglomerates like Disney, Sony, Bertelsmann, Viacom, AOL Time-Warner, Vivendi, and General Electric. The majority of these multinational companies have an interest in each facet of the industry—film, music, publishing, radio, new media.

However, you can still find thousands of jobs at smaller, independent firms. There are nimble film and TV production companies that may work with big networks and distributors. Plus, some publishing imprints, record labels, and film production companies operate like independent houses, even if they ultimately report to a larger corporation.

Salary

MBAs should expect to take the "entertainment industry haircut"—that is, lower pay in exchange for the excitement and glamour of the industry. Fresh out of business school, you should be able to start at $70,000 to $80,000, depending on the position.

Hours

In general, the actual on-the-clock hours will not rival the insane schedule required by most investment banks. Many insiders reported relatively humane days, beginning at 9:30 or 10:00 A.M. and ending at around 7:00 or 8:00 P.M. There are crunch periods, usually at the beginning or end of the year or around deadlines, where 12-hour days are not uncommon.

Travel

Although some industry executives make frequent trips between New York and Los Angeles, positions usually do not require heavy travel since the majority of the business is conducted in these two cities.

Office Culture

"Absolutely whatever" is how one record-company vice president described the dress code. She was wearing red thigh-high boots at the time. Indeed, next to the technology sector, there are few industries that take the concept of "corporate casual" to such an extreme. It's not unusual to see CEOs padding around the office in jeans and sneakers. Still, casual is not the same as slob, and at entertainment companies you'll be expected to look hip.

The Crowd

One of the great perks of working in the entertainment industry is that you are invariably surrounded by smart, fun, hip, talented people. This is a business grounded in charisma—and you will be valued for yours. Most people have a bachelor's degree, and many will have more advanced degrees—but don't expect them to be overly impressed with your MBA. Despite the billions of dollars that are at stake, this is still a very anti-corporate culture.

Getting In

Move to New York or Los Angeles. While there are certainly opportunities at regional newspapers and local television affiliates, if you want to make it big in this industry, you're going to have to move to one of the coasts. And network. Because they have a surplus of wannabe employees, M&E companies don't do a ton of recruiting. That's why networking and developing contacts is crucial if you want a job in this industry. Be persistent, and have a thick hide. "If people don't return your calls, it's because they're busy, not because they don't like you," says one insider.

INTERNET/NEW MEDIA

Overview

Five years ago, the Internet was most likely a very marginal part of your life. Today it probably plays a role in almost everything you do—shopping, research, communication. The latest industry innovation—wireless technology—has made it even more pervasive. Cell phones and PDAs are now becoming Internet-enabled.

In early 2000, the prospect of big payoffs, along with the desire to be a part of this new industry, was still inspiring many MBAs to reject corporate jobs and join Internet firms. A year later, they'd begun flocking back to traditional companies. There are still job options out there—just not as many. The trend now is hiring more experienced managers—many with MBAs.

Major Players

The industry has evolved quickly, but several players have managed to show some staying power, among them ISP to the masses AOL; power portal Yahoo!; auctioneer eBay; on-line broker E*Trade; on-line ad agency DoubleClick; e-commerce giant Amazon; and software behemoth Microsoft.

Salary

Not surprisingly, salaries vary widely among Internet companies—variables include industry segment, size, stage (pre-IPO or public), and location, among others. But on average, MBAs can expect to make $70,000 to $110,000, plus options.

Hours

Working at a dot-com is almost never a nine-to-five job, but it rarely demands the round-the-clock madness of start-ups. Most of our contacts in the industry report that they work about 60 hours a week—maybe a few more during the occasional crunch period—and that their schedule is relatively predictable.

Travel

Travel is extremely infrequent, with most respondents reporting that they never travel. A few say they travel two to four days a month.

Office Culture

Even as the surviving dot-coms mature into more established companies, they manage to maintain the casual feel of start-ups. Office atmosphere and meetings tend to be laid back and unstructured, and dress codes range from "none" to "business casual." Cubicles or open office space are the norm at space-starved Internet companies, with few, if any, private offices.

The Crowd

Bright was probably the word most used to describe dot-com coworkers, with *motivated* and *fun* close behind. The male-female ratio is usually pretty even in the Internet world, except in tech departments or at highly technical firms, which are still generally male-dominated.

Getting In

MBA jobs range from marketing to finance to business development. Internet (or e-business) consulting is also an important trend right now, and many of the big consulting giants now include an Internet division. (See Consulting) There's not a lot of B-school recruiting going on in this industry. Almost everyone we spoke with reported having been referred to his or her current employer by a friend, so networking is the name of the game.

Find out as much as you can about the company and its competitors so that you can offer some insight into the company's market. During the interview, be sure to stress that you'll be a good fit—highlight flexibility, a solid work ethic, and creativity.

One invaluable tip: Be prepared to explain one great accomplishment that produced tangible results, even if it was in a completely unrelated field. Dot-coms are looking for adaptability, leadership, and problem-solving skills.

START-UPS

Overview

The emergence of the Internet in the mid-1990s destroyed many of the barriers to entry that new businesses traditionally faced. By using the Web, entrepreneurs could immediately establish a global presence, quickly overcoming the limitations of geography with minimal expense. Unfortunately, actually turning a profit isn't quite as easy as start-up founders and venture capitalists hoped, and once investors realized that, Internet company stocks took a pounding. It is now harder to get VC support. Though money is still available, VC firms are much more discerning, looking for profitability sooner and for more seasoned management teams.

Salary

Recent MBA grads will find that salaries at start-ups can be somewhat lower than in other fields, but then again, the potential payoff from options could more than make up for the smaller paychecks. In general, MBAs right out of school can expect $80,000 to $100,000, plus options.

Hours

The legendary 20-hour days do exist, but they don't seem to be as common as they once were. Of course, no one's clocking out after 8 hours, either. The average tends to be about 60–70 hours a week.

Travel

Depending on your role in the company, travel varies considerably—anywhere from 10 percent to 50 percent of your time might be spent on the road. On the whole though, you're much less likely to be subjected to the rigorous travel schedules common in banking or consulting.

Office Culture

Relaxed, casual, and *laid back* appeared over and over again in our surveys. Nearly all the people we spoke with professed that they enjoy the low-key atmosphere, casual dress code, and frequent socializing that seems to be the norm in the start-up scene. It's not all fun and games, though. You've likely heard the tales of foosball tables and Ping-Pong tournaments in hip offices of start-ups. What you might not have heard is that these toys relieve stress in an extremely intense environment. It's sink or swim for these young companies, and members of a start-up's team feel that pressure keenly every day.

The Crowd

The employees are a pretty varied group, depending on the type of company. Some firms are packed with MBAs; others have just one or two in their ranks, with plans to add more as the company grows. That's partly due to the fact that pre-IPO companies can't compete with more established firms when it comes to salary and benefits. Also, in the current market climate, many risk-averse MBAs are deciding to stick with the stability of established companies.

Getting In

There's definitely good news and bad news here. Bad news first: According to startupseekers.com, 80 percent of start-ups fail by their second year. Joining a start-up means embracing the very real possibility that your stock options will end up worthless and your job will disappear. The good news is that the pay is reasonable and start-ups need qualified people—especially MBAs and anyone with industry experience. If you fit the bill, your chances of finding a job at a start-up are pretty good. Roles for MBAs at start-ups include marketing, business development, finance, sales, and management.

New companies hire almost exclusively through internal contacts and word-of-mouth, so tell everyone you know that you'd like to work for a start-up, check out your school's alumni database, and attend launch parties and other networking events whenever possible.

A surefire way to get a top job at a start-up? Found your own company. Short of that, many get positions because they knew the CEO and/or founders, and some were recruited by friends within the company. Though very, very few jobs are advertised, the web site start up seekers.com promises to match start-ups with qualified job seekers. Glocapsearch.com helps candidates find positions at new Internet and tech firms.

VENTURE CAPITAL/PRIVATE EQUITY

Overview

Venture capital firms invest their own capital in companies in exchange for a generous share of stock and future profits. They often get equity stakes of 20 to 40 percent of the business. Their end goal is to help build a strong company and drive it toward a liquidity event like a merger or IPO. In the '90s, VC firms began to invest in burgeoning Internet companies, and equity financing soon surpassed debt financing as the entrepreneurial model of choice. A slew of successful IPOs fueled the VC fire—1999 saw more than $35 billion in venture-backed investments, significantly more than ever before. And despite the "dot-bombs" of 2000, last year's venture capital investments were still the highest in history.

Major Players

The ten VC firms with the largest portfolio investments for 1999 (according to PWC's Money Tree Survey):

Accel Partners (Silicon Valley's Sand Hill Road)
Sequoia Capital (Sand Hill Road)
Oak Investment Partners (Palo Alto, California)
Mayfield Fund (Sand Hill Road)
New Enterprise Associates (Sand Hill Road/Baltimore, Maryland/Reston, Virginia)
Chase Capital Partners (New York)
Bessemer Venture Partners (Massachusetts)
Norwest Venture Partners (Palo Alto)
U.S. Venture Partners (Sand Hill Road)
Draper Fisher Jurvetson (Redwood City, California)

Others of note:

Kleiner Perkins Caufield & Byers (Sand Hill Road)
Internet Capital Group (Wayne, Pennsylvania)

Charles River Venture Partners (Waltham, Massachusetts)
Venrock Associates (New York City)
Benchmark Capital (Sand Hill Road)
Barksdale Group (Sand Hill Road)
CMGI, Inc. (Massachusetts)

This is not an easy industry to break into. Most VC firms employ MBAs, usually from top schools like Harvard and Stanford. Many of those MBAs also have degrees or professional backgrounds in technical fields like software, telecommunications, or health care. The combination of business/finance experience and technical prowess is a winning one in this industry.

Salary

In the VC/private-equity world, compensation is broken up into salary, bonus, and carried interest. Salaries generally range from $100,000 to $200,000, and bonuses are usually greater than the base salary. Basically, carried interest is the profit split of proceeds to the general partners.

Hours

The norm is 60–70 hours a week, though it varies from firm to firm and from project to project.

Travel

If you're at a VC firm on Sand Hill Road, most of your clients are also in the Valley and you travel infrequently. Venture capitalists elsewhere in the country might travel one to two days each week.

Office Culture

Most VC firms range in size from 5 to 15 people, so the atmosphere is quite intimate. One insider describes the mood as "mature, intense, highly professional, and discreet." Dress is generally business casual. Though the hours aren't as intense as those in investment banking or some consulting positions, people work diligently, and lunches are often spent in front of a computer.

The social life in VC firms isn't like that of an investment bank or a typical Internet start-up. It is a close-knit environment, but there aren't as many happy hours. It isn't an industry that most people break into right after college, like consulting or investment banking, and "work hard, play hard" is definitely not a mantra you hear at VC firms.

The Crowd

This is not a business for the faint of heart. The stakes are high and you must be willing to take risks. Although venture capitalists are always zealous about performing due diligence on potential investments, "gut instinct" is also a factor in every decision. You have to trust yourself and your business savvy. The VC world is not the most diverse, and women tend to be scarce. Many firms still have an "old boys' club" atmosphere.

Getting In

What's your best shot? It's all about networking. The chance of getting a job by sending in a resumé and cover letter is very slim. Get in touch with undergraduate or B-school alumni in the business, meet as many people as you can, and make an impression. VC firms will rarely go to schools and interview. If they do, they are guaranteed to have hundreds of students vying for one or two positions. Don't expect trick questions or cases to be thrown at you in an interview. These intimate operations depend on good chemistry between employees, so you should expect to meet every professional at a firm.

HIGH TECH/TELECOM

If you want to work with the hottest, newest gadgets—and if you thrive in a fast-paced, competitive environment that offers plenty of opportunity for swift advancement but will be around long enough to make a meaningful contribution to your 401(k)—a tech company could be just what you're after.

Many Old Economy firms are frantically trying to remake themselves as future-savvy egalitarian institutions. In an industry based on innovation, companies are continually vying to be the first to uncover the Next Big Thing. Hot concepts right now include third-generation wireless technology, palmtop computers, Internet appliances, broadband Internet access, and server-centric "rented" application software.

And then there's Linux. The open-source operating system has attracted major public interest and corporate investment in recent years. The main strengths of Linux are its scalability (the OS runs on hardware ranging from wristwatches to supercomputers), stability (Linux systems have been known to run for years without crashing), and low cost (Linux itself is available for free, and companies like Red Hat and

SuSE distribute reasonably priced optimized packages). In February 2001, IBM president and COO Sam Palmisano declared, "Linux is ready for real business."

San Diego, Silicon Valley, Austin, Seattle, and New York are predictable hubs for technology firms, but biggies (especially older companies) are scattered all over the country—Motorola's headquarters are in the Chicago suburb of Schaumburg, Illinois, and Corning, New York, is still home to the eponymous company.

Major Players

In an industry of this scale, major players generally concentrate on a subsector rather than the full spectrum. Microsoft has a virtual monopoly on desktop operating systems. Oracle is a key player in the database arena; Apple, Borland, Red Hat, Corel, and a slew of other companies work in the OS and application space. Gateway, Sony, Micron, Sun Microsystems, Apple, IBM, Toshiba, and others build PC and server hardware. Dell ranks number one for office desktops, while Sun Microsystems dominates the server market. IBM is the world's top manufacturer of supercomputers, the heavyweights used by brokerage houses and universities to make complex calculations. Internet infrastructure is provided by the likes of Cisco, Corning, Lucent, and JDS Uniphase. AT&T, Sprint, WorldCom, and Verizon are major telecom players; in wireless, they're joined by Qualcomm, BellSouth, Nokia, Ericsson, Siemens, and others. (Nokia makes wireless handsets; Qualcomm owns the patents on one of the major wireless networks in the United States.)

Salary

With the reality of stock option riches fading, tech-industry job applicants are focusing on straight salary. Generally, you'll find that salaries start at $70,000 and up, depending on the size of the company, what it does, and where it's located.

Hours

This is an intense industry for intense people. "It is always crunch time," one product manager said. You'll probably work a reliable 60 to 70 hours a week, with the time commitment sometimes increasing as you move up.

Travel

Depending on your job, work-related travel is relatively common at a tech company. Product managers, marketing managers, and business development managers all reported traveling about one week a month. This industry depends on customer contacts, especially in this shaky economy.

Office Culture

Cubicles, cubicles, cubicles. There are even cubes at old, staid firms like AT&T—though companies that didn't start out as computer firms have higher chances of offering offices or open-plan layouts. Among the cubicles, though, there can be a definite sense of camaraderie and even fun; software companies are the most extreme example, with free food and other perks. Behemoths Intel and Microsoft provide soda and (in Microsoft's case) basketball hoops in some offices.

In the past, these companies tried to play hard as well as work hard, with company-sponsored beer fests or happy hours. These are becoming less frequent as expenses are being trimmed.

Dress is usually casual or "office casual." At major firms including IBM and Lucent, though, marketing and biz-dev staff, who have direct contact with corporate clients, still sport suits.

The Crowd

High-tech workers reported their colleagues to be bright but sometimes competitive to a fault. Though the sector boasts an ethnically diverse population, women tend to be heavily represented, especially in marketing.

MBAs in this industry work in management, business development, product development, and marketing. The more diverse your educational background—the more technical, especially—the more routes are open to you.

Getting In

This is an industry full of personality and product cults, so know the technology—and if possible, become part of the cult. Several of our insiders said that interview questions focused not only on the company's technology but also on industry competitors; so read the latest trade publications. And don't rely on monthly magazines, which can be behind the times in this fast-paced business. Scour the Web (*ZDNet*, *CNET*, and *Upside* are some of our favorites) for the latest headlines, and keep up with what's happening.

HEALTH CARE/BIOTECHNOLOGY

Overview

Far from being a single industry with clearly defined producers and buyers, health care comprises a complex web of stakeholders: insurers, "payers" (public or private entities that pay for health-care costs) and regulators; hospitals, pharmaceutical firms, and device makers; physicians and other health-care professionals; and consumers. Over the past two decades, the major trend has been the introduction of managed-care organizations (MCOs) and other mechanisms to rein in skyrocketing costs.

Recently, thanks to consumer and political pressure, MCOs and other payers have loosened the leash, allowing greater patient choice and physician autonomy. Costs are on the rise again, but now the emphasis is on controlling expenses and boosting quality, often by bringing new technologies and business strategies to bear on traditional health-care organizations.

Meanwhile, hundreds of biotechnology and device companies are vying to introduce the next billion-dollar drug or must-have device (or, in some cases, combinations of the two). While the drug development industry has a high failure rate—most prospects never make it out of clinical trials—dozens of drugs each year survive the grueling process of clinical testing and FDA approval.

Introducing these products can be a challenge worthy of the most aggressive marketer. Because of their tight cost environment, providers are skeptical of new technologies. New technology also requires additional training that may be difficult to schedule with heavy patient loads, and payers—always the 500-pound gorilla in the room—may resist shelling out more money.

Salary

Salary depends on many factors: the type of company or institution you join, the specific job, and other degrees or experience you bring to the table. Those from a middle-tier B-school with a health-care concentration who join provider or payer firms can expect around $50,000 to $60,000 to start. Pharmaceutical and device companies offer starting salaries of $75,000 to $95,000.

You also have the option of working for the health-care practice of a consulting firm or in an investment bank. These positions typically pay $80,000 to $110,000; higher salaries go to those who graduate from top schools or have additional relevant degrees.

A dual degree can give you an automatic salary boost. A Ph.D./MBA generally garners $100,000 and up; an M.D./MBA, about $125,000 to $150,000 and up at most organizations.

Hours

Working hours will depend on your specific job and the particular industry segment in which you work. If you work in finance at a hospital or in marketing at a pharmaceutical firm, you might have standard business hours. For those in consulting, 55 to 75 hours a week is the norm. Those who work with venture capitalists or in investment banks also work 50-plus hours a week. Naturally, at a development-stage biotechnology or device firm, you'll have all the excitement—and long hours—expected at a start-up.

Travel

The amount of travel varies tremendously from job to job. A consultant may spend fifteen or more days on the road each month, while a hospital CFO travels only rarely. Those in health-care venture capital or business development might spend up to 30 percent of their time traveling.

Office Culture

Health-care culture tends to be conservative, particularly at the corporate level. Business attire is the rule, although many offices have adopted casual-Friday policies. At a start-up, the dress code is more casual. Consultants usually dress formally at the client site or for client meetings, but business casual is the rule on Fridays at the home office.

The Crowd

Everyone working in health care has to learn how doctors think. Physicians are the gatekeepers of health care and interface with virtually every other segment of the industry. Their decisions determine whether a new drug is a billion-dollar-a-year blockbuster or one of several $100-million-a-year also-rans. Their willingness to comply determines whether a cost-savings guideline will be fully implemented or largely ignored. The bottom line is that you must achieve physician buy-in to effect change in health care.

Because health care is such a large industry—one-seventh of the U.S. economy—it is diverse. Health-care workplaces, whether at the corporate or delivery level, bring together smart people from many backgrounds, although many of the traditional gender and race divisions remain: You won't meet too many male chief nurses or managers of home-care operations, for example.

Index

MBA JUNGLE

EDITOR-IN-CHIEF *Bill Shapiro*

CREATIVE DIRECTOR
Matthew Guemple

DEPUTY EDITOR *Kendall Hamilton*

MANAGING EDITOR *John Dioso*

SENIOR EDITOR *Robert Dunn*

SENIOR EDITOR *Geoffrey Morris*

EDITOR AT LARGE *Jon Gluck*

ASSOCIATE EDITOR *Ryan D'Agostino*

PHOTO EDITOR *Ondrea Barbe*

EDITORIAL ASSISTANT *Alexis Offen*

CONTRIBUTING EDITORS
*Anne Dunham, Justin Heimberg,
David Jacobson, Karen Kozlowski
(Fashion), Jeff Ousborne,
Paul Scott, Jim Thornton, David Wallis,
Russell Wild*

ART CONTRIBUTORS

*Peter Berson, Bob Eckstein, Michael
Edwards, Johanna Goodman, Tom
Haynes, Jens Mortensen, Peter Stemmler*

CHIEF TECHNOLOGY OFFICER
Oren Wortman

DIRECTOR, ONLINE CONTENT
Suma CM

DEPUTY DIRECTOR, ONLINE CONTENT
Jenny Bailly

CREATIVE DIRECTOR, ONLINE MEDIA
Courtney Skulley

DIRECTOR, USER EXPERIENCE
Kenneth S. Fassman

SENIOR WEB DEVELOPER *Aviv Roth*

WEB DEVELOPER *Joe Carbe*

WEB DEVELOPER *Dina Smoykhet*

PUBLISHER *Lawrence C. Burstein*

ASSOCIATE PUBLISHER *Gail C. Day*

ADVERTISING SALES DIRECTOR
Jeffrey Greif

ACCOUNT MANAGER *Brian Irving*

ACCOUNT MANAGER *Mark E. Lipson*

ACCOUNT MANAGER *Daniel McIntyre*

LOS ANGELES SALES OFFICE
SD Media, Corey Spiegel
(310-264-7575)

SAN FRANCISCO SALES OFFICE
SD Media, Jennifer Tatko
(415-925-6600)

DETROIT SALES OFFICE
Heth & Associates (248-642-7273)

DIRECTOR, BUSINESS DEVELOPMENT
James Winter

MANAGER, BUSINESS DEVELOPMENT
Peter Lallas

MARKETING ANALYST
Marina Selepouchin

VICE PRESIDENT, SALES
Jennifer Lemaigre

DIRECTOR, SALES *Roland Lange*

DIRECTOR, SALES *Dan Silvert*

MANAGER, SALES *Jaime D'Amico*

OFFICE MANAGER *Alex Carberry*

JUNGLE INTERACTIVE MEDIA, INC.

Co-Founder   *Jon Housman*

Co-Founder   *Jonathan McBride*

Co-Founder   *Sean McDuffy*

COO   *Lawrence C. Burstein*

Director, Finance
Michele S. Blair

General Counsel
Gunderson Dettmer

Public Relations
*Four Corners Communications
(212-849-8250)*

Advisory Board:
*John Berg, Jeff Bernstein, Jim Borth,
George Daly, Bill Grimes, Jacob Hill,
Elie Housman, Kevin O'Malley,
Julius Sarkozy*

E-mail:
*advertising@mbajungle.com,
editors@mbajungle.com,
subscriptions@mbajungle.com*

Many thanks to
*Steven Audi, John Beauclair,
W. Stewart Cahn, Ellie Cornish, Peter
Dunn, Robyn Fruchterman, Philip
Getter, Marian Gibbon, Godfrey Gill,
Robert Gold,
Rosalie Goldberg, Leslie Wolff Goldin,
Jay Hachigian, Richard Hesp,
Sean Kelly, Justin Lunin-Pack,
Doug McNeely, Gregory Miller, Susan
Miller, Elizabeth Murray, Noreen
Murray, Faris Naber,
Randy Rock, David Sharrow,
Joshua Shaub, Lawrence J. Weissman*

JUNGLE INTERACTIVE
MEDIA, INC.
10 East 18th Street, Eighth Floor,
New York, NY 10003
866-4JUNGLE
www.jungleinteractive.com

Subscriptions: 1 year (8 issues):
U.S. $12.00; Canada $18.00;
international $27.00.

For queries and customer service,
call 866-251-0840 or go to
www.mbajungle.com.

For high-quality article reprints,
contact Reprint Management
Services at 717-399-1900.